Miami

Midlife

Joseph Dunn

Newleaf

Newleaf

an imprint of
Gill & Macmillan Ltd
Hume Avenue
Park West
Dublin 12
with associated companies throughout the world
www.gillmacmillan.ie

© 2001 Joseph Dunn
0 7171 3272 2
Design by Vermillion
Illustration by Emma Eustace
Print origination by Linda Kelly
Printed by ColourBooks Ltd, Dublin

This book is typeset in Rotis Semi Sans 10pt on 13pt.

The paper used in this book is made from the wood pulp of managed forests. For every tree felled, at least one tree is planted, thereby renewing natural resources.

A catalogue record is available for this book from the British Library.

5 4 3 2 1

To Susan

CONTENTS

CHAPTER 1

INTRODUCTION

No one warns you about it. You don't see it coming. It drifts in, like a fog off the sea, to envelop you. One day you just find yourself in the middle of it. Sometimes it takes a tragedy, like divorce or depression, before you realise you're there. It's called midlife. It's a time of extraordinary turmoil, like a second adolescence. It's a mental storm, like a ten-year epileptic fit. If your teenage hormones gave you hell, brace yourself: your midlife restlessness will do the same.

That's what this book is about: how to prepare for, understand and deal with those awful years between the ages of thirty-fivish and fiftyish. If you're under thirty-five, let this book serve as a warning. Forewarned is forearmed and all that. If you're over fifty you can rest on your wrinkly old laurels and chuckle about the life hurdles you've successfully jumped. If you're between those ages, start reading and don't stop until the back cover comes into view. It might save your marriage and your sanity.

Unfortunately I'm in this last category: smack bang in the middle of this second puberty. Nasty stuff. But it gives me an opportunity to record some of my own observations. What's more, I'm a psychiatrist (strange job but someone's got to do it), so I've accumulated a wealth of observations about other people's experience of midlife. I'm hoping I've learned enough lessons to pass on a few insights. You can be the judge.

In this book I'll start with the heavy stuff: disillusionment. It's one of my favourite topics. Disillusioning experiences are like phallic symbols: once you know what they are you start recognising them everywhere. And midlife is, above all, a phase of surrendering one's benign fantasies about how great life will be when you've got life experience, a secure relationship, money in the bank and seniority at work. Somehow, none of those things seem that important any more and your career has become a millstone. Your whole value system begins to shake at its foundations. Then I will launch into the whole body-mind-spirit thing, with some practical hints for staying healthy and avoiding the divorce courts.

After that I will dwell on the morbid subject of death, since no one younger than thirty-five has any true concept of what that means. We older folk do: that's why we sell our motorcycles, buy cars with airbags and envy anyone who has the nerve to jump out of a perfectly good aeroplane (or tie elastic around their ankles and step off a bridge). With thoughts on death go just as many thoughts on meaning. As in *the meaning of life.*

Finally, after all these ponderous thoughts I will give you the good news: there's life after midlife! If you play your cards right, this post-midlife (I dare not call it *old age*) can be the best time of all. Just enough years to pack in some thoroughly egocentric pleasure-seeking before your pelvic organs, that you used with such mastery in your junior years, finally pack it in. Also, in post-midlife your task is to achieve the state of mind that has eluded you for decades. It's called 'peace'. If your current worries are paying the mortgage or where your next dirty weekend is coming from, you don't have it. If your angst is about your credit card debt or the young Turks at the office who are vying for your role, you *certainly* don't have it. But if your perspective on life is one of retrospective self-congratulation, the pleasure of grandparenting and a calm embrace of the inevitability of your own end then you've got it in bucketsful. So hang onto it.

With respect to the writing I have used a few techniques developed in my previous books, such as a 'Consider this' paragraph, an 'Exercise' for you to do or else a 'Case history'. Please note that, in the case histories, any resemblance to any individual, living or dead, is purely coincidental. And here's the first exercise:

Exercise

Now you've sailed through the introduction, what next? Simple.

1. If you're standing in a bookshop trying hard not to bend the crisp cover of the book, all you have to do is take it up to that nice person behind the counter, surrender some money (thanks, I could do with the royalties) and take this book home in a brown paper bag.

2. If, on the other hand, you've found it in a library, put it back on the shelf and go find a bookshop that stocks it (thanks again).

3. If you've found it on your friend's coffee table and you're so young you're worried about your credit card debt, I hereby give you permission to borrow it from your friend, on condition that you never give it back. If your friend declines to lend it to you, just steal it behind his or her back. That way he or she will have to go back to the bookshop and get another copy.

4. My gratitude overflows ...

CHAPTER 2

MIDLIFE & MIDDLE AGE

Midlife. First, let's try to define what it is. I'll start with what it's *not.* It's not middle age. Sure, they sound similar, but allow me to make the distinction.

Middle age is a concept dreamed up by demographers with obsessional personalities. Middle age is the time between the ages of forty and sixty. There, diabolically simple. Slicing our lifespan up into twenty-year portions satisfies people like statisticians, census-takers, researchers, etc. But we all know they're a peculiar lot who are stuck in the anal stage of their development. They like precision and black-and-white certainty. Machiavelli would be proud of their compartmentalising ruthlessness. What a pity people just don't fit so nicely into their divisions.

Midlife, on the other hand, starts around thirty-five years of age but some precocious developers might start the slide in their early thirties. Having a particularly difficult life (trauma, loss, grief, tax audits) matures one a little early too. Some others who, say, have been cosseted from the realities of life by being filthy rich might hit midlife several years later. As you can see, it doesn't start at midnight on the night before your fortieth birthday, much to the consternation of scientists who were severely potty-trained.

The point at which midlife stops can be similarly vague. I'll come back to that notion towards the end of the book. But the principle applies that midlife, like adolescence, is a unique, idiosyncratic experience that no two people experience identically. Just as we look back at how some of our friends endured pubic hair and pimples without alarm, so some people seem to wander through midlife unscathed. Well, almost unscathed. In some way, for everyone, it's a time of blowing away our existential cobwebs.

Also, keep in mind that men and women experience midlife in dramatically different ways. In the traditional (currently politically incorrect) roles of hunter-gatherer versus nurturer, midlife might mean finding oneself trapped in an uninspiring but lucrative job on the one hand, or an empty nest on the other. Female menopause is far more obvious than its male equivalent. Women experience more depression, but men jump off more cliffs. Men experience their wives' infidelities as a narcissistic injury, while women whose husbands screw around are most confronted with issues of trust and betrayal. Men run out of heartbeats earlier than do women, etc., etc.

I'm also all too aware that I've been cursed with a 'Y' chromosome (but also blessed with the magnificent reproductive apparatus that that involves) so I'll do my best to be 'P.C.' as I record these words. But please bear with me if you find yourself reading a passage that smacks of a male bias. I'll try not to think like a man. If, in fact, thinking is what men do.

Now here's an odd thought: midlife is actually the second of three life crises. Don't panic at the thought. Most of you have already endured the first of these and the last one's more of a getting-near-the-end retrospective, an unwritten autobiography.

Consider this

You're twenty. You know it all. Or at least you think you know it all. You thought you knew it all when you were sixteen too, but now you're four years, two heartbreaks, umpteen exams and a driver's licence wiser. And what a relief to discard your virginity. It was becoming some sort of sexual albatross flying around the ship of your adolescence.

You're pretty cool. All the teenagers in the street look up to you. You can rest assured that they'll always be younger than you. More junior. You see, being older is good. Being older is having more street-cred. Your own clothes, your own (for want of a better word) hairstyle. Even a grotty flat downtown if you can afford the rent. You can share it with an alcoholic university student, a guy who's never told you about his stint in prison and a budding heroin addict. Independence. Ah, life is good, even if you subsist on fish and chips.

But there's a problem that lurks in the back of your mind and comes to haunt you in your quieter moments. What are you going to do with this life of yours? After all, you're supposed to be laying down the foundations for your future. You know, a career, a stable relationship, an income to get you away from this troglodytic flat and the drunk, the criminal and the needle-jockey some day.

So this is your first life crisis: early adulthood. The question you ask yourself is '*Who will I be?*' Also, for some reason, at this time of your life you want to be *older* ...

Now consider this

You're forty. Naughty forty. You thought you knew it all when you were younger, but the older you get the more you realise how little you know. You don't so much have a career as a ball and chain. The bank very kindly lets you live in the house they own. All you have to do is watch large amounts of your income disappear at regular intervals. Sometimes when they send you the bank statements they appear to have run out of black ink and replaced it with a rather nice shade of red.

You have teenage kids. They think they know it all and they try to convince you that you know nothing. You agree.

But you envy their naïvety, their self-confident optimism (born out of their ignorance) and the suppleness of their youth. You wish you could turn back the clock, but take what little wisdom you've acquired with you. If you knew then what you know now ...

You're aware that your joints are stiff in the cold of the morning. Perhaps that's because you're first out of bed while the teenagers snooze on in that garbage tip they call a bedroom. One day, as you gaze out of the window on a drizzly day, you wonder what has become of your life. Why did you ever want to be older when now you'd dive back into youth like Free Willy? If you look externally as if you now have some power in life, why do you feel so feeble? Somewhere, beneath the layer upon layer of excrescences that have barnacled the hull of your life there resides an inner core of true you, if only you could find it again.

Welcome to midlife. Now you want to be *younger*. And the question you're asking yourself is '*Who am I?*'

Now consider this

You're seventy. Heavenly seventy. You know a bit and you've long since accepted that you never did know it all, nor will you. You're just grateful for the bit you know.

You went to see that nice young doctor (he's only fifty) last week and he did a biopsy on a lump on your back that's been bleeding. Bad news. You've got cancer. The Big C. Death, where is thy sting? It's on the end of the needle the doctor used to give you a local anaesthetic.

You've been carrying it for years, this nemesis of yours. Feeding this bad bit with your perfectly good blood. But then, why not? It might be evil but it's still part of you. Your tissues, your genes, gone wrong. Of course you were shocked. You went home and cried. Haven't done that for years. Long since lost the need. But now you've re-learned the art of weeping. You're allowed some self-pity, given the circumstances. You make the nice young(ish) doctor promise he won't skimp on the morphine when your time comes. He's so glad to agree.

This is your getting-near-the-end crisis. Facing your inevitable end. It's just as well you went through that midlife crisis. It was hellish at the time, but you learned some valuable lessons as you struggled through. You re-learned to love your spouse. You found some sense of meaning in this life of yours and the beautiful world you've lived in. You rediscovered something in your life that was divine and ever-present. That'll be handy now.

In quiet moments, when your kids have taken their kids and gone home, you find yourself re-examining your life under a microscope of memories. You don't particularly want to die but then you don't particularly want to turn back the clock either. Not much sense in going back to where you've been already. Just as well you managed to find peace and acceptance in your last few decades. No, you must move forwards. Take the plunge. You grasp for that divine touch again.

The deathbed crisis, perhaps. You don't want to be older or *younger* now. You just want to be where you are for as long as that lasts. The question you keep coming back to is '*Who was I?*'

∞ ∞ ∞ ∞ ∞ ∞ ∞ ∞ ∞ ∞ ∞

Get my drift? Life is two steps forward and one step backwards. But midlife is a huge stumble. So hang onto the good news: once you've survived midlife you can survive just about anything ...

CHAPTER 3

FANTASY & DISILLUSIONMENT

Still not sure what midlife is? Let's define it in terms of fantasy and disillusionment. You see, all through life we entertain a number of fantasies about it. Life, that is. Our fantasies are the cuddly rug of our unconscious mind. They're there to comfort us, like an adult teddy bear.

When I use the word 'fantasy', what image does this conjure up in your mind? What's your fantasy of fantasy? I expect it involves some very attractive person slowly removing every stitch of clothing. Or a sensual embrace accompanied by what romance novelists call the 'throbbing urgency'. Perhaps it involves a group of the aforementioned attractive people who seem to be experiencing some difficulty keeping their hands off you.

You wouldn't be alone if you thought all fantasy was erotic. No, they're just the nicest of fantasies. There are plenty of other fantasies and they tend to metamorphose over life. Case in point. Let's consider some twenty-something fantasies. The kind that don't involve simultaneous orgasms ... They might be:

- reaching the pinnacle of your career and being admired and envied by all;

- being surrounded by loving friends and family who resemble the Brady Bunch;

- cruising Main Street in a red con
  everything;

- the auditorium applauding as you're award

- MGM phoning you again to double their previous
  to do the lead role in the next blockbuster, alongside
  or starlet of your choice.

Quaint, aren't they? We sometimes slip back to the old ways,
but in midlife our fantasies assume a rather different complexion.
In my work as a psychiatrist I've encountered them again and
again. There are seven common midlife fantasies, as follows ...

Fantasy #1: To flee

You want to flee. More than anything else you just want to throw
down your rifle and run from the battlefield. Or your briefcase and
run from the office. Or your ring and run from the marriage. Or
your kids and run from the crushing responsibility of loving them.

You start pricing real estate at some sleepy hamlet a few
hours' drive from town. You fantasise about the simple life, never
admitting to yourself that you'd just be replacing one prison for
another: the smothering office block for the gross under-
stimulation of your hamlet.

You're so crowded in. You've lost yourself, your identity, your
individuality. You wear the uniform of your career. You walk the
walk and talk the talk. You no longer have a name, just a rank and
serial number. You've become a worker ant, no longer important
in your own right, just there to swell the crowd. Pretty soon
you've bumped into Fantasy #2 ...

vertible with chrome-plated

d your doctorate;

offer for you

the star

he mountains. Or in the
hermit instinct emerges.
yearn for a life devoid of
on your belt goes off one
to a thousand diodes. If one
you you're going to pretend
Babel and you have no idea

a rainy day you suddenly come to understand ⋯ ith machineguns suddenly snap and clear their paths of a ⋯ innocent strangers. It's because they're there. In your face. When the next sleepy commuter bumps your elbow he or she is going to cop a mouthful of sarcasm and a withering look.

In your idealistic twenties you used to worry about the overpopulation of the Third World. Now everywhere you look there are people, people, people. Not even another round of Bubonic plague will fix it. The shack in the sand dunes looks like nirvana.

Fantasy #3: To regress

They're called 'Sugar Daddies', although plastic surgeons are aware that there's a female equivalent. They find themselves in midlife and don't like it one little bit. The prospect of hurrying up their development and careering into old age doesn't appeal so they only have one escape route: backwards. They try to look and act younger than they are.

Sugar Daddies find pretty early on that the girls they're attracted to are not attracted to them. Unless, of course, they have some sort of father complex because their own dads left their lives years ago and Mr Sugar here looks like a suitable replacement. Or they're working girls and Sugar pays them for some passionless groping and to act out Sugar's ghastly fantasies. Or they're gold diggers and Sugar's a good earner. Enough loot to hang around for a year or two and enjoy holidays in the Bahamas. Or perhaps they've realised that boys of their own age are about as mature as a green banana and seem to use only three per cent of their brains at any one time. Anyway, Sugar Daddies learn early on that they can't pull the chicks unless they do something with their appearance, and so they use a few 'props' as part of their act.

They go down to the hairdressers and get the latest cut along with lashings and lashings of black hair dye. They emerge looking ten years younger, if it weren't for the wrinkles. So they undergo the agony of some cosmetic surgeon poking a few syringefuls of collagen into their faces and convince themselves they don't really look like dyed, puffy old men.

Then the props. Just as well Sugar earns a lot, because he's going to have to make the diggers know he's got gold. First, there's fulfilling the adolescent fantasy of the red convertible with the chrome-plated everything. And a Harley Davidson to make him look a like a rebel without a clue. Then the threads: tight jeans and the latest trinkets, all in fashionable black (when, oh when will that trend every end?). And then there's the gym membership, which Sugar will take out for a year but use only twice ...

Then he has to be seen in all the right places. So he hangs

around in nightclubs where the ultraviolet lighting makes every blonde in the room instantly locatable. He's not really looking for the working girl or the gold digger: he wants to track down the sweet young thing whose dad bolted when she was five. Putty.

When he finds her he'll take her to the most expensive restaurants and compensate for his expanding girth by wowing her with luxury. He feeds into her fantasy and she into his. The businessman and the bimbo. His failing sexual performance is countered by his ability to walk into the yacht club with this sweet young thing. He's demonstrating to crony friends that he's still got It. And she's demonstrating to all the other sweet young things that she can pull a rich guy like this.

At this stage, please accept my heartfelt apologies for the unbridled cynicism expressed above. But I suppose we all know someone like Sugar. Don't we?

So is there a female equivalent of this male regressor? Of course there is. She's called Mutton Dressed As Lamb. Her favourite cosmetic surgeon has put silicon bags inside the parts of her that are supposed to protrude and sucked the innards out of anything that's not. The skin on her face looks as if it will only stand one more 'lift' before it snaps. She actually believes all those mythical cosmetic advertisements about how some perfumed cream will make her look younger. She's got an eye for the toy-boys and she knows how to prop up a bar where they drink. Not so much Narcissus as Narcissa ...

But within the hearts of Mr Sugar and Ms Mutton there lies a deep fear. The fear of being old, ugly, alone. It's a fear we all possess, but in midlife this is expressed in the saddest of ways ...

Fantasy #4: To get back to nature

There's a little bit of Pol Pot in all of us. He's the murderous nutcase who wiped out every Cambodian intellectual and wanted to re-create the agrarian society. Sure, we don't really harbour plans for a genocidal infamy, but we sometimes gaze out of the office window on an eternally overcast day and imagine what it would be like to run a little strawberry farm. Planted around that little shack we're going to get in the mountains. The one without the telephones or faxes.

Our fantasy involves the sound of wind in the trees and bleating lambs. Picnics on a crisp, sunny day at the flat paddock down by the river. Cheery hospitality in a country pub.

No mention of the months of winter mud. Nor that the wildlife is more rats than ravens. Nor the financial reality of sending the lambs to the abattoir. Let's not let those clammy realities burst the bubble of this delightful dream. A type of regression too, I suppose, just like Sugar's and Mutton's. A devolution into idealising the simpler societies of past centuries. We like to think they must have had an easier life, but our romance blinds us to the realities of poverty and young mothers dying in childbirth.

Fantasy #5: To create

At work you're an expert on Policies and Procedures. Your desk is lined with manuals. If X happens, then staff are supposed to work through steps 9 to 12, except in the last month of the financial year, at which time step 11 should be replaced with ... etc. If there's a dispute, there's always a dusty old 'P and P' manual to resolve it.

It certainly beats your last job, which was filing. You got to be able to recite the alphabet backwards in your sleep. Did Mr Williams' file come before Mrs Williamson's? Of course. Follow the rules. It's all so inflexibly simple.

You gaze out the window. The image that comes to your mind doesn't involve the shack in the mountains. It's more the literary prize. Within you beats the heart of a thwarted writer. No, poet! As yet undiscovered. An unknown Shakespeare in the suburbs. One day there'll be a brass plaque with a silhouette of your head (post-facelift) attached to the wall of your house for all to see. You lived here, it'll say, until such-and-such a year. Before you accepted that laureate role. Or the honorary professorial chair in literature.

Or what about turning those dabbled attempts at painting into something that could grace the walls of the Louvre? You'll pass etchings on to grateful nieces and nephews, telling them they'll be more valuable after you go to that great Studio in the Sky. Yes, painting, that's the way to give vent to this lurking creativity that now rests heavily in your heart. Already, like Picasso, you can feel a *blue period* coming on.

A common midlife fantasy. Born out of our years of repressing our creative urges. Why? Because we have to conform, that's why. For heaven's sake, if we were all oozing creativity who would be left to write Policy and Procedure manuals!?

Fantasy #6: To explore

In your youth you did the hippy trail through South-East Asia, then a rattly Third World aeroplane to India before taking in the pyramids, dodging some small arms fire in the Middle East and a few months working in a bar on the Greek islands. Your worldly possessions could be fitted into a backpack. You came home to a society of pasty-faced writers of P and P manuals who didn't have the slightest interest in your holiday snaps.

If you never did this sort of exploring in your youth, you're bound to start feeling the restlessness in midlife. Even if you did do the hippy trail, you'll still be recurrently drawn back to the exploring fantasy. Neil Armstrong, Ed Hillary, Chris Columbus and You. Anything to get away from these damned P and P manuals. Yeah, born to be wild. Lead on, my biker friend.

I suppose that in midlife you're supposed to be able to explore again, but this time in a bit more comfort. No more cockroaches and malaria. No more being searched at border posts by gentlemen with no sense of humour. No more wiring your parents to send lawyers, guns and money. Now, with graying temples and gold credit cards, you can do it on an ocean liner and spend most of the exploration drinking mango daiquiris around the swimming pool. Or inspecting the pyramids as you fly into Cairo, business class. 'I wonder what all the poor people are doing today?', you think to yourself as you check yourself into the Ritz. In the slummy, Third World streetscape from your hotel room window you quickly learn exactly what they're doing: trying to stay alive. Poverty sucks. The credit card goes a long way to compensating for middle-aged spread and gout.

It also gives you some wings to fly. Away from the manuals and payslips. Away from your balding boss and his bad temper. Midlife, more than any other time, is when you must broaden your horizons. Or re-broaden them if your backpack has sat too long in the back of some mouldy cupboard. So get on with it ... Finish this chapter at the airport departure lounge.

Fantasy #7: To find meaning

Once, many years ago, you had a passion for your P and P manuals. Now, in midlife, they all seem like such drivel, pap, trivia. You held your political ideals with such conviction. Now all the politicians seem like crooks. Your goal was to pay off your mortgage. Congratulations. But why does that not fill you up? Why are you not basking in your financial security because you'd hoped that that last mortgage payment would make you feel complete? So what's missing?

Then, an awful thing happens. Someone you love dies. You watch the ashes being scattered. How could this beautiful, living, breathing person be reduced to so much nondescript powder? Not so long ago you embraced her and felt her warmth and vitality. Where did she go? She must be somewhere other than in this gray dust; the sort of residue you'd sweep out of your grate at home after a cosy night of story-telling in front of the fire.

You've never really touched death like this before. It gets you thinking. For the first time you truly realise you're going to end up all ashen one day yourself. Scary thought. You shudder. And think some more. So what's it all about, this life of yours? You have some sense of identity and direction. You have a purpose. But meaning, that's different. Not so much *who* you are, but *why* you are.

If you ever find out, let me know, would you?

Case history

Some years ago I treated a patient who had a Ph.D. in philosophy. Not geothermal engineering. Not 18th century literature. Not acid secretion of the canine stomach. She had the real thing. She was a Doctor of Philosophy in philosophy.

I apologised to her in that I was aware she had come to seek my advice, but would she bear with me and answer one brief question before we got on with dealing with her panic attacks? She was rather taken aback, but immediately agreed. So I asked her the question on everyone's lips: What is the meaning of life? She looked at me as if I was a complete idiot and answered without hesitation: Well, there are plenty of them ... all you've got to do is choose one.

I pondered momentarily. The answer was spot on, but still rather unsatisfying. We got on with talking about panic attacks.

MIDLIFE AS DISILLUSIONMENT

As you can see, fantasies are like bottoms: we've all got them. But in my work as a psychiatrist I encounter a variety of people who have lost their fantasies in a crushing way. The traumatised (who had the fantasy of being safe), the abandoned (who had the fantasy of secure love), the bereaved (who had the fantasy that we all live forever). According to the psychiatric textbooks I'll diagnose them as having post-traumatic stress disorder, or grief or depression. But those labels paint only half the picture. I like to peel back the layers of their fantasy and examine how it was propped up by their denial until it fell, like a house of cards. Fragile things, fantasies.

Ponder, for a moment, how the human mind predicts the future. It oscillates wildly between optimism and pessimism. In the extremes of these oscillations lie diagnosable types of psychopathology.

Consider this

You're depressed. Everything's bad, black, negative. You despise yourself, you pathetic creature. You see everyone's failings, but mostly your own. The world is a nasty place full of war, famine and disease. You can't stand watching the television news because it's mostly bad news. You despair. Not only will the future be no better, it'll almost certainly be worse. What's the point in going on? A distant cliff beckons.

Now consider this

You're manic. It used to be called 'manic-depression' but it's been reborn as 'bipolar disorder'. The former sounds a little too mad, but the latter a little too clinical. Who cares? When you're as high as a kite, everything's just marvellous anyway.

Your thoughts race and brim with uncharacteristic creativity. You're on a roll, expansive, grandiose. Life couldn't be better. You try to telephone the Pope but get cut off by a rude telephonist at the Vatican. You check into a five-star hotel and order French champagne on room service. God bless credit cards! Your libido is rampant and you've got the herpes to prove it. The world is your oyster and the future couldn't look better. But somewhere in the back of your mind a little warning bell is going off and you're trying hard not to hear it. You've been here before and you know that any day now you're going to crash into the blackest of beckoning-cliff moods. So live for today. This delicious, sunny, manic day.

Now consider this

You've got GAD. That's Generalised Anxiety Disorder, to the uninitiated. How does it manifest itself? You worry too much. You worry about the future. You worry about more than one thing at a time. You know you worry too much and that this spills over into muscle tension, insomnia and irritability. You try to use your cognitive strategies to overcome this negativity. Just look at all those things you worried about before and how many of them actually happened. Not many. You say this over and over. Sometimes it helps you to get a better perspective on things. Often it doesn't. The future seems, well, *unsafe*.

Now consider this

You're a compulsive gambler. Your life runs in cycles of hope and despair. When you put some money down on a horse you have fantasies of instant, easy money. The trouble is that the horses you follow like to follow other horses. Somehow, you shrug off the despair and look for another lame nag to rest all your hopes on. You live in a world of denial. Denial that you're losing money so fast that you and your family's financial future is slowly going down the gurgler.

∞ ∞ ∞ ∞ ∞ ∞ ∞ ∞ ∞ ∞

Now these images of optimism versus pessimism are, of course, extremes. Most of us have milder, but just as real, sentiments of hope and despair. In the darker end of the pendulum's swing is that vague feeling of sad dissatisfaction with life. It lives within us all, even those with the sunniest natures. Philosophers call it the *Human Condition*. To Christians it's *Original Sin*, projected on us all by our naked ancestors in the Garden of Eden, and all because of a talking snake and a piece of fruit. Freud called it '*normal human sadness*'. I call it the ERB feeling, which stands for *Empty Restless Boredom*. For obvious reasons.

Buddhists call it Dukkha, and it relates to the first of the four Noble Truths of that philosophy. It's usually expressed as 'life is suffering', but that misses something in the translation. Dukkha means *disillusionment*. Again, the loss of a pleasurable fantasy. And the other three Noble Truths state that disillusionment comes from putting our hopes and fantasies into things and people, all of which will disappoint us. And the sooner we can forsake these human needs the happier we'll be. Suddenly the image that springs to my mind is me trying to push a camel through the eye of a needle ...

Now here's an odd thought. Research shows that mildly depressed people see the world the way it is! The rest of us live in a mild state of benign denial. Or at least until the sinewy hand of reality takes hold. Once you cotton on to this feeling of disillusionment you come to realise just how much it's part of life.

Consider this

You're wildly, passionately in love. Your lover can do no wrong. No matter how much pillow rub he has in his hair in the morning, he's still beautiful. Even when he's angry he's cute. Making love is seventh heaven.

Run! Flee now, while you have the chance! Don't you know that falling in love is a type of temporary insanity foisted upon us by hormones that just want to copulate? Can't you see that those odd little habits that now seem cute will one day irritate you?

In seven years' time, while your two toddlers are being looked after by your mother-in-law, you'll dart glances of pure venom at each other across the aisle of the divorce court. Erotic love. The most common disillusionment of them all.

Post coitum omne animale tristis est. (After sex every animal is sad).

Now consider this

You're going through one of those questioning times in life when you meet some absolutely charming people who belong to a spiritual group. They give you all the answers you ever wanted, and far more than my patient with the Ph.D. Slowly but surely, you become embroiled in the group and come to idealise the saffron-robed guru who is their leader. A bottomless well of wisdom. You hand over all your worldly possessions because, after all, material things are just going to give you more Dukkha than you can cope with.

When you finally escape from this cult you'll end up drowning in your disillusionment. You've been conned, preyed upon because of your vulnerability. Just like that nice man in the Eighties who took your money with a promise of returning it fourfold in three months and now lives in a mansion in Mustique ...

Now consider this

You're going to sue someone. Get the bastard. And get justice at the same time. It's all so easy. Your lawyer fires you up, like a sergeant-major leading his men over the top of the trench. Once more into the breach, dear friends, and there's a big fat cheque when we annihilate the enemy lines.

It's only when you have your day in court that the disillusionment sets in. You thought that Justice and the Law had something in common. But the Law is about how to define words contained in dusty old manuals, just like the P and P ones at work.

You start to wonder what your lawyer would look like in saffron robes. Another common disillusionment experience.

And now consider this
You're pregnant. Male readers may have to stretch their imaginations, and their abdominal muscles, to slip into this image.

You've never been pregnant before and your mind is filled with images of your baby looking cuddly and adorable. You're going to go through this labour drug-free because that's what the other women in your ante-natal class are going to do too. Somehow you've bought into that old myth about how women in the Third World just squat under a palm tree to give birth and then go back to work in the fields. You're planning to go easy on yourself and return to work after, say, three months.

It's second trimester. Things are going swimmingly. You touch that deep sense of calm and purpose that only pregnant women in mid-trimester can experience.

A few months later you go into labour. You scream for pethidine. Your baby's head is stuck in a pelvis that was designed more for disco dancing than being split apart by Satan's spawn. When you awake after the Caesarean section you greet your baby for the first time. It looks less like the baby in the nappy advertisements and more like the Creature from the Black Lagoon. You take it home. It doesn't sleep. It cries loudly enough to be heard by the Child Protection Agency. You struggle on, trying hard to love it, but increasingly aware of why post-natal depression occurs after ten per cent of deliveries.

∞ ∞ ∞ ∞ ∞ ∞ ∞ ∞ ∞ ∞

Now let's recap. What I've focused on in this chapter is the notion that human beings thrive on fantasy but must handle disillusionment. In early adulthood one's fantasies usually revolve around wealth, power, fame, status, security and love. In midlife most of these apparitions fade. Poverty may buy misery but money doesn't buy happiness. With power comes responsibility and shoulders that bend under the strain. Erotic love is blissful but illusory; real, plodding, ambivalent love is hard work.

So in midlife we replace them with a different set of fantasies: to flee, to isolate, to create, etc. But the Buddhists are right. All fantasies are just bubbles waiting to burst. We create prisons of responsibility with our jobs, our debt, our relationships and bringing up our kids. *The only choice we have in life is which prison we're going to live in.* Think about it.

Only in midlife can we surrender some of our worn-out fantasies and come to peaceful terms with what life is and what it isn't. If this chapter is enough to make you hearken the call of the beckoning cliff, take heart! There's a wonderful life after midlife, and all you have to do is hang on …

CHAPTER 4

CAREER

Midlife is a time to rethink one's career. We start them, like love affairs, with energy and optimism. Somewhere early on the shine wears off and they become a bit of a drag. Disillusionment is alive and well and poisoning the workforce. Routine, commuting, Policies and Procedures manuals. Endless, tedious, pointless, badly run meetings. Answering to the idiots above you. No wonder workers' unions were formed: to channel the shared disillusionment into a united voice of anger. What about the worker?! And management, themselves burned out and gazing at the beckoning cliffs in the distance, become the brunt of all this frustration.

So by way of a quick guide through this mire of problems, let me introduce you to the Seven Truisms of Work. I suppose that 'truism' is a grandiose title. Judge for yourself, but I'd like a sound counter-argument before I admit they're falsisms.

Truism #1: You stand on the glass floor

In the height of the feminist movement there was much discontent about something that came to be called *the glass ceiling.* The idea was this: you're climbing the corporate ladder to success when suddenly your head hits something hard and invisible. Much as you try you just can't get to that next rung up the ladder. Why not? Because you're a woman and the people hanging out on the next rungs are all, you guessed it, *men*! Corporate sexism. Keep the womenfolk in middle management or below. Keep the boardroom on the forty-somethingth floor for the Old Boys. No admittance without school tie!

But are those Old Boys happy with all their power? They seem to drink a hell of a lot, they die five or ten years too early and every so often they're tossed out onto the scrapheap. School tie or not, no one likes a Captain of Industry when he's fat and fifty.

The guts of this truism is that *with authority comes responsibility*. Just ask the management consultants. In the lofty field of job design, they work according to a strict formula: if you have responsibility for some part of the company you must have power to make decisions about it. Conversely, if you're given authority you must be accountable for what you do with all this power.

Suddenly the power of upper management becomes a bit of an illusion. Our Captain of Industry started life with a fantasy (there's that word again) that he'd climb this ladder to the top. When he got there, it would be like standing on top of a mountain. He'd have power over all he could see and all knees would bend at the mention of his name. Today, Allied Plastics; tomorrow, Microsoft!

But his spoonful of Dukkha tastes like hemlock. It comes with the realisation that there's not really a whole lot of fun or indulgence at his level of the ladder. In fact, it just feels like a whole lot of hard work. He finds himself dreaming of being able to opt out (Fantasy #1: to flee!) Or down the ladder again to a height that's not so vertiginous. He doesn't really need all this income. He works such long hours that he goes home in time to have dinner and go to bed. His teenage kids hardly know him anymore and his wife has had her sexual needs met by the man who cleans the swimming pool.

But there's the catch. The family complain about his absence but they rely on his income. He's trapped. There's no climbing down, just out. And if he leaves this cruel corporate game there's no coming back. The power he has is a hot potato; he'd love to pass it on to someone else. He might be gazing out of the forty-somethingth floor window, but his mind is captivated by the image of a little shack hidden among the sand dunes of a deserted beach. No telephones, no faxes, no e-mails. Sounds familiar?

To some extent we all end up standing on the glass floor in midlife. We'd love to smash it into a million shards but then we'd just fall. I wonder how many coffee shops and news agencies are being run by the Humpty Dumpties of the corporate world ...

Truism #2: Workaholism is both a trap and an escape

Mostly men again. Sometimes a man will indulge his workaholism because it's an escape. Sure it's a trap at the same time, as described above, but it's his own chosen prison. Rather poignantly, it's because he feels more comfortable at work. The office, after all, is a structured environment. It runs on P and P manuals. The language is of goals, hierarchies, rules, modes of communication. Clean and unambiguous.

But when our Captain goes home it's a different story. His wife long since stopped trying to communicate with him. The man who cleans the swimming pool has not only a fantastic physique, but also a sense of humour. The Captain had a sense of humour once, many years ago, but he left it behind when he was promoted out of middle management. Now the only dialect he can speak contains words like 'price-earnings ratio' and 'fully franked dividends'. The Captain's pimply son is surly because he has an aching father-hunger that his father just can't see. The Captain's daughter has tried heroin once and wishes she hadn't. Now she knows how good it is.

Workaholics usually display characteristics of the obsessive personality: rigid, inflexible, perfectionist, controlled and controlling. Lots of 'shoulds' and self-imposed rules. Great with the fine details, but no concept of the Big Picture of life. Unable to delegate because no one would do the job to their own high standard. Got any Captains in your life?

But the sadness of the Captain's existence is that he's lost some part of himself. Just like women who lose their identities in abusive relationships. The Captain appears to have lost some part of his soul. I think he sold it to the company store ...

Truism #3: The corporate world is emotionally violent

It masquerades behind chrome, formica, leather, oak boardroom tables and business suits with criminal pricetags. It looks good but it's skin-deep. Go and find a city office that's been gutted for renovation: it's just gray concrete waiting for some extortionist interior decorator to apply a veneer of sophistication.

Make no mistake: the corporate world is just a jungle inhabited by savages with laptop computers. They value refinement, like who can tell the wittiest jokes over boozy lunches and whose silk tie cost enough to feed an African village for a week. But when it comes to greed, back-stabbing and naked ambition, their suits look like loincloths and their ties like garottes.

To Freud it was all about the Oedipal struggle and the size of one's penis. In the jungle it's more like the size of your club: kill or be killed. Kill or starve. Whatever you do, keep killing and make sure it's not one of your kinsmen or you're next. It's easy to romanticise the Noble Savage but I've practised tropical medicine in countries where violence is part of life and there's no constabulary within a hundred kilometres. Walk through the corporate world as if you're in Zambia. And look out for predators in the undergrowth.

Now a few thoughts on office politics. Don't even dream that you're ever going to find an office where it doesn't happen. It's part of the executive-eat-executive corporate world. Wherever you enter a workgroup you'll find the same dynamics at work. Freud held that the family was the prototype for all subsequent human systems and he's got a point there. There are recurring problems within any system of hierarchy, power struggles, miscommunications, victims-and-rescuers, etc. You'll always find the office idiot, the office gossip, the self-righteous grizzler, the passive-aggressive personality, the melancholic, the arrogant twit, the drunk, the letch and the timid person who consistently avoids promotion, to name but a few. Now remember this little motto: *swim in office politics and you'll drown*. It's part of the jungle that is any company. When you enter a new job, tread softly until you've sussed out who fills which role in this game. Hold your cards close to your chest and take nothing and no one at face value.

In the workplace a little bit of paranoia goes a long way.

Truism #4: Money doesn't buy happiness but poverty buys misery

How much income is enough? Being on the bones of your backside is no fun, but wearing your backside out sitting at your workstation doesn't seem a great idea either.

Be wary of the Parkinson's law of income. You may have heard of the original Parkinson's law, which stated that 'a task expands into the time allowed for it'. With apologies to Parkinson, my own observation, expressed in plagiaristic terms, is that '*your expectations of lifestyle expand into, and beyond, your income*'. If you earn X pounds or dollars, you'll always need X + 1. If you get a raise to, say, X + 10 pounds or dollars, you'll end up needing X + 11.

When is enough really enough? Money, after all, doesn't buy happiness. It just buys choices and lifestyle. Like restaurant meals, private schools and men to clean the swimming pool. But then, sexual gratification aside, we can do without all those things, can't we?

Now here's another odd thought. When industrial researchers study the factors that contribute to job satisfaction they invariably come up with a startling finding: staff aren't really concerned about how much they're paid. They just want to know that they're being paid equitably, so that other people on their rung of the ladder who do more or less what they do receive X as well. They are severely disillusioned if they find they're actually on half-X. In the satisfaction stakes, money doesn't rate very highly at all. Other, subtler, more human factors come into play. Being respected. Having their contribution valued. Being heard and getting an injection of empathy when they're unhappy. Friday drinks after work and a drunken Christmas party to kick off a few torrid affairs in the photocopying room. Money comes a long way down the list.

On a morbid note, let me tell you about a friend of mine who died in her thirties of cancer. A few months before she died – and before she was too confused by morphine – we shared a Deep and Meaningful conversation. She said to me, 'You know, I used to worry about money. Now all I worry about is time.' These days, when I get my bank statements and find the bank has run out of black ink again, those words ring in my ears.

Truism #5: These days, everyone has at least three careers per lifetime

Gone are the days when you signed on with the company at fifteen and got a gold watch at sixty-five. Just look at your own career and that of the midlifers you know. You start with a Bachelor of Something degree, then go into an insurance company. That's too boring so you go overseas, dodging the small arms fire in the Middle East and end up smuggling some hashish you bought in a coffee shop in Amsterdam. When you come back to your homeland a friend offers you a directorship in a company he's starting. Three years later you find your friend has been embezzling all the profit.

After a messy fraud investigation and liquidation you go back to university to finish your Master's degree in Something Else, which you finance by bar work at the local pub, before taking up a great opportunity in the 'dot.com' world. Then the bottom falls out of that market so you try your hand at selling real estate while secretly working on the best-selling novel you're writing in the dark of night (but which will never see the light of day). Shortly after this, your mother-in-law takes pity on you and employs you in her wholesaling business but this stresses your marriage because, after all, your mother-in-law is a consummate bitch.

By now you're into the world of parenthood and mortgages. You're also getting awfully midlifey around this time and on the point of going all alternative (you know, little shack in the sand dunes and all that) when you notice an advertisement for a highly-paid job for someone with a Master's degree in Something Else. You're perfect for the position and hang onto it just long enough to score a handsome redundancy package after the next stockmarket crash. This takes you nearly to retirement age but your old bones are still limber enough to renovate a couple of houses and build a block of flats in their backyard.

Then to the fantasy of retirement which you're sure will be just like twenty-six two-week holidays strung back-to-back through the year (but ends in the disillusionment of being boring as hell).

Oh, and I forgot that short stint of bus-driving.

By my calculations, that's about ten careers. You deserve a prize for what, in the current jargon, is called *multiskilling*. But you rather envy people who get the gold watch at sixty-five.

Truism #6: Plus ça change, plus c'est la même chose

I hope that's not Franglais. It translates as 'the more things change, the more they stay the same'. By this I refer to theories of business and management. They come. They go. Another one comes. For a while. Then it's replaced. With every new theory there is a rush of enthusiasm. The shelf-life for a new trend in management? About five years, I suppose. They're always greeted with wild enthusiasm and then abandoned, like a cast-off lover, with a healthy dose of Dukkha. In our culture obsolescence no longer applies simply to cars.

The cycles go on. Boom and bust. Bear market, bull market. Expansion, consolidation. Hiring, firing. Old ideas wrapped up in new packaging.

And a thought about managerial skills. Pardon my bias, but isn't a good manager born, not made? Can you learn the sort of personality that makes a good leader at business college, or isn't this something that started in your genes, was nurtured by loving parents and ended up with you becoming the school captain? Leadership, after all, is something expected from below, not imposed from above.

Truism #7: Everyone needs a sabbatical

When I was a university student (so many decades ago I shudder!) this was the province of the professors. Every seven years or so they'd be given a year off, fully paid. Gratis. Supposedly to further their own education, but I always wondered how many of them studied sunbathing in Biarritz. Or wine-making in Tuscany. What a fantastic idea!

So I got to thinking. I try not to do this too often because it strains the gray matter, but sometimes an idea just falls into your cranium from the heavens above. Or perhaps it surfaces from somewhere in the murky depths of your unconscious mind. So here's the idea: why don't we all take a sabbatical? There. I said it. Disturbingly simple, don't you think?

I suppose it's just a more constructive form of Fantasy #1: to flee. Also Fantasy #6: to explore. And what about Fantasy #3: to regress? Now that's not such a bad deal: three fantasies for the price of one.

It's not so nutty, because after I've fled and got my midlife head together, I'm planning to come back! I'm preparing for my sabbatical already. I've got too many financial responsibilities just now, mostly in the form of children, so I can't flee just now or my bank manager would come after me. But in a few years' time I'll be off. Just for three or six months or so. Part of my fantasy is to fit my worldly possessions into a backpack – or a camper van – and wave the rat-race goodbye. I've invited my wife to come with me, but we're into a sad case of fantasy-clash here, so her response is 'write to me often' ... That's okay, I've still got a few years to work on her. If only Gucci made backpacks!

After all, what's the alternative? To work fifty weeks of the year for fifty years? And then to retire at an age when I'm too weary and arthritic to dodge small arms fire in the Middle East? Not for me. You only get one chance at this life, reincarnations excepted, and it must be an awful experience to climb into your deathbed with a regret that you didn't take the opportunity to leave the rodents behind and drink in as much of this beautiful world as you possibly could. If you take nothing else from this book, take this: plan a sabbatical at some stage in your career. Do it in midlife. Promise yourself. Make yourself do it. Fortune favours the brave. And the stupid. Be a bit of both.

I look forward to meeting you on the road. How does Marrakesh sound?

CHAPTER 5

BODY

Now that you've got your career sorted out, let's examine your body. It's that other aspect of your existence that you take with you wherever you go. Even to Marrakesh.

Midlife is, after all, when we get confronted with the inescapable effects of ageing. Everything moves south: not just breasts, but facial tissues, bellies and a half a dozen internal organs you don't even know the names of.

So let's forge on. We'll start with beauty, which starts to dwindle in midlife. Or does it?

∞ ∞ ∞ ∞ ∞ ∞ ∞ ∞ ∞ ∞ ∞

BEAUTY

Exercise

1. Open a fashion magazine. Any fashion magazine. Now check out the models, both male and female. Aren't they drop-dead gorgeous? Wouldn't you just love a night, just one night, of unbridled passion with the stunner of your choice?

2. If the answer is 'no' I suggest you consult your physician forthwith. There's something wrong with your hormones. Either that or you're so post-midlife you've run out of fantasies.

3. Now consider the following questions. Just how old are these nymphs and nymphets? In their teens, I'm afraid. Just what proportion of the population look as good as they do? One, two per cent perhaps? The rest of us are plain, plain, plain. See? Statistically, beauty is quite, quite abnormal.

4. Now go to a fashion show. Sneak around the back to where the models hang out. The fridge in the dressing room is bereft of food but stacked with diet soft drinks. That's fifty per cent of their diet. The other half is comprised of cigarettes and cocaine, both of which are also calorie-free. What proportion of the population is size ten? Again, being bulky is normal. It's these stick figures who are the freaks.

5. Now go home and throw away all your diet books and gym equipment. You're way too old to be a stick figure.

You really know you're finishing the midlife phase when you can step out on the beach in a swimsuit and not give a damn what anyone thinks of you.

Consider this

You're beautiful. Gorgeous. Ninety-eight per cent of readers will just have to bend their imaginations with this particular image.

So let's have a look at your lifestyle. First, to stay a stick but avoid a cocaine habit, you have to spend most of your waking hours hungry. Certainly, after years of practising for the next world famine, your stomach shrinks a little. But not much. You could still tuck into a burger and fries at just about any moment of the day. And round it off with an ice cream sundae.

Next, whenever you meet a M.O.T.O.S. (that's Member Of The Opposite Sex, for short ... gay readers can translate this as M.O.T.S.S.) they won't have the slightest interest in your mental prowess, your life experience or your ailing mother. They just want to take your clothes off. Gorgeous people have a lot of trouble being taken seriously.

Then there's your exercise regimen. And you know all too well that if you stop this self-imposed torture it'll only take a few days before those firm muscles assume the consistency of custard.

You might be adored by masses of M.O.T.O.S's but you'll be despised by jealous hordes of M.O.T.S.S's. You must be really looking forward to midlife, when you can bulge in that swimsuit and tuck into that burger.

See? Being gorgeous is a blessing at times but a damnable curse at others.

Now consider this

You're male. Female readers may have to temporarily shut down various portions of their brains in order to get into this image. Like the parts that generate speech and emotion. Also that little supervisory bit that tells you you've had too much to drink.

Not only are you male, but your hairline, like a spring tide, has receded to the nether regions of your pate. In other words you're balding and it's not going to be too long before you look like a dildo with ears.

So what do you do? You grow one side of your dwindling hair supply long and every morning you conscientiously comb it over the shiny bald bit. You look at yourself in the mirror and convince yourself you look a little less bald.

Brother, have you got it wrong! You just look like a bald guy who's desperate to look festooned with hair. Do yourself a favour. Can the comb-over. Burn your toupee. Tear out your hair transplant. Take pride in that expanse of shiny skin. Polish it daily. After all, you can't grow grass on a busy street.

DIET

Exercise

Complete this multiple-choice question:

The five food groups are:

(a) fruits, vegetables, grains, dairy products, meat;

(b) celery, mung beans, lentils, brown rice and raw anything;

(c) salt, fat, chocolate, gin and tonic.

If you answered (a), you're a shameless know-it-all. If you answered (b), it's about time you gave up this hippie lifestyle and tucked into a large steak and chips. If you answered (c), you're a genuine midlifer and it's about time you had a good long look at your diet before the chest pain strikes.

I won't try to offer advice on diet. It would be hypocritical. Mine consists of the items named in (c). I'm waiting for the chest pain. I suppose I look upon food as being one of those little consolations, there to enjoy like a Sunday morning sleep-in. I wouldn't be anorectic for quids.

Trot off to see a dietician.

EXERCISE

I'll start the section on exercise with just that, an exercise:

1. Drop to the floor and do twenty push-ups. Make sure no one's watching apart, perhaps, from your personal nurse who's carrying the resuscitation equipment. There's nothing more humiliating than people giggling as you work out.

2. If you make it to one and a half push-ups you're a midlifer. Ten push-ups and you're nothing but a show-off. If you make twenty, you're certainly too young and fit to be a midlifer but you'd better read on so you can learn what's just around the corner for you.

3. The lesson to be learned is that in midlife you have to do most things, like push-ups, in moderation. Approach exercise like Goldilocks looking for a comfortable bed to sleep in: not too hard and not too soft. Buddhists call it *walking the middle road*. Diet and exercise, you see, have to be a *lifestyle*, not a *project*. They become an automatic part of your day, everyday. Not something you'll be doing for the next four weeks.

4. The Divine Designer of your over-ripe body has blessed you with two pieces of apparatus that'll make all that gym equipment redundant. They're called *legs* and like Nancy Sinatra's boots (oops, showing my age there) they're made for walking. That's the exercise that's most appropriate for midlifers. Not sweating on a *pec-deck* at the gym. Not clambering over unnamed peaks in some heathen country.

Just walking, twenty minutes a day, five days a week. A lifestyle thing, not a project. So go and walk that Buddhist road. But be aware that it's supposed to be the middle road, not the middle *of the* road. Otherwise you'll get run over. And that's not good for anyone's health.

But now, another confession. Personally, I prefer to follow the Oscar Wilde school of exercise: whenever I get the urge to exercise I just lie down and take some deep breaths until it passes over ...

MEDICAL CARE

As your youthful agility becomes a poignant memory you're going to have to confront a disturbing thought: you need a good doctor in your life. Of course, part of your hippyish regression in midlife may be to explore all of the unorthodox aspects of healthcare, like acupuncture, homeopathy or chiropractic. But when that chest pain informs you of the sorry state of your coronary arteries, I doubt that you'll be calling for your herbalist.

So here are some handy hints. Most countries, with the exception of the US, run a two-tier health system in which roughly half of all medical graduates become general practitioners and the other half become specialists. The biggest priority is to find a good G.P. Then hope and pray that he or she knows all the good specialists.

The best way of finding a good G.P. is by personal recommendation, so if you've moved into a new area the best advice is to ask as many locals as possible about the doctors in the district. Then go and check out one of the front-runners. Avoid doctors who are too young (knowledgeable but inexperienced) or too old (experienced but out of touch with the latest). Find someone who's like you: in midlife.

See whether you feel comfortable with that person, whether he or she talks to you in language you understand and seems to make sense. See how expensive that person is and how accessible, particularly after-hours when that chest pain arrives. With the exception of the oddities of the British National Health Service (take that last word with a grain of salt) there's nothing to stop you changing your G.P. if your initial impressions turn out to be delusions.

We live in the days of consumer rights. Gone is the era of 'doctor's orders' and I can reassure you that we doctors are rather relieved by that trend as well. We are, like all professional consultants, merely advisors. You pay for our advice and you can choose whether to accept and act on it or whether to tell us to go jump.

You can always ask for a second opinion. In fact I often ask my own patients to go and get a second opinion from a colleague if I'm stumped or my treatment isn't working. If your doctor gets huffy and offended by such a request it's about time you found another doctor.

Finally, be patient with us. After all, that's why they call patients *patients*. Do you know everything there is to know about your own chosen career? I doubt it. Neither do we doctors. Medicine is getting harder and harder. There's more and more to know. Medical specialities are fragmenting into sub-specialities. In my own field you now get general psychiatrists, forensic psychiatrists, psychiatrists who are psychoanalysts (leather couch and all), child and family psychiatrists, public psychiatrists, private psychiatrists, psychiatrists who work in community health centres and chase schizophrenics around, biological psychiatrists who love playing with pills and electro-encephalographs, etc., etc. You get the picture. We doctors can't know it all. But don't be afraid to ask questions anyway.

And expect an answer that's not laced with doctor-speak.

CHAPTER 6

MIND

If this book were being written by a dermatologist I'm sure this chapter would be about skin care in midlife. If a gastroenterologist were the author, you'd be reading now about liver, colon, number twos, etc. But me, I'm a psychiatrist. A shrink. So here's my indulgence: a chapter on your mind. Ponder it carefully. Your mind's the most valuable apparatus you've got. Certainly more precious than anything at the opposite end of the torso, even for aficionados of horizontal folk dancing.

I'm going to hold forth on mind problems because I see people develop a whole range of mental symptoms in midlife. And the greatest problem is that *most of them go undiagnosed and untreated*. People simply live with the torture of this fear or sadness for years. They're often unaware that their torment is described in my textbooks and, in the course of my day-to-day work, I see people blossom after years of misery. Also, I'm all too aware that we psychiatrists have a bit of an image problem. People still think most of us really do have leather couches. I know of not one single male colleague with a goatee beard. Rather than being intense mind-readers we're just ordinary Joe (or Jo) Blows in the suburbs. You could walk past us in the supermarket and never realise. That's because you still think we all look like Sigmund Freud.

So here's my attempt to give you a crash course in mental

problems of midlife. And to overcome the ignorance and stigma as well. If you identify with any of the (fictitious) case histories below, you'd better make an appointment to see that nice G.P. you found after reading the last chapter.

DISILLUSIONMENT

Done it already. But read on and you'll encounter some text on depression. That's because if you cop too much disillusionment in life you start sliding into a black hole.

SENESCENCE

This refers to the fact that your gray matter starts to get rusty as you age. Not only do you lose physical agility but the mental athletics that characterised your school and university years seem to have wandered away. You just can't remember such long shopping lists and your kids beat you at mental arithmetic. You find yourself going to a room at home but being unable to remember what you went there to get. You have to check the street map again at every traffic lights, just to make sure you know where you're driving.

But fear not. This is usually a benign condition and might not even get to you in midlife. It becomes more of a nuisance in your sixties. It doesn't necessarily mean you're moving into Alzheimer's or some other hideous brain disorder, just that you're not twenty-one anymore and the nerve cells in your brain have known better days.

With one caveat: failing mental function, especially

concentration, decision-making and short-term memory, can be a cardinal sign of depression. In fact in midlife, the rust that infects gray matter is *usually* depression. And that's one of the nastiest conditions of all. Read on.

REGRET

Je ne regrette rien. That's what Edith Piaf, the warbly French chanteuse, used to sing. It means 'I regret nothing'. Oh, that we should be so lucky. Most of us don't regret *rien*, we regret plenty.

In midlife, as part of our 'Who am I?' phase, we start to review our lives. We survey not only the successes and triumphs but also the things we've stuffed up badly. The insults we blurted out. The times we failed our loved ones. The sure-fire investment schemes promoted by a charming chap who currently lives in Majorca. The premarital sexual adventures we missed out on because we were too young and silly to recognise a 'come hither' even if it was shouted at us through a megaphone. To name just a few.

So midlife must become a time of self-forgiveness. Even though we psychiatrists just love to live in the past ('so why do you hate your mother?') we're the first to admit you can't change your past. Only your present and your future. Narcissistic personalities forgive themselves far too easily. Sociopathic personalities don't have a problem with self-forgiveness because they seem to lack that part of the mind that generates guilt. But for most of us, self-forgiveness is an art form that needs to be learned and practised regularly. The worst people at this are the obsessional. The who? The obsessional. Keep reading.

OBSESSIONALITY

A bit further on in this chapter I'm going to describe obsessive-compulsive disorder. All this terminology can become confusing, so let me state up front that I'm referring here to obsessionality as a personality trait, not an anxiety disorder. Have faith. This should all become clearer as you struggle through this chapter. I'll kick off with an illustrative case history.

Case history
Norman was obsessional. Most truly obsessional personalities are male but women who try to think like men can become just as crippled if they try hard enough.

Norman was precise to the point of being boring. He set high standards for himself and nothing was going to let these self-imposed rules bend. Control was the name of the game. Self-control to the point of self-flagellation. Control of others in true dictatorial style. Sounds familiar? You read about the Normans of this world in Chapter 4 when I was musing over the Captain of Industry.

My points here are threefold:

■ Obsessional people are too rigid. They're perfectionist, judgmental and racked with guilt and regret. To the moralist, their conscience has been stuck in overdrive for too long. To the psychoanalyst their superego, that unconscious repository of rules and regulations, is pumping out too many messages of self-criticism. To the neuroanatomist the frontal lobes of their brains have been pumping too many electrical impulses. Any way you look at it, these people have to chill out.

■ Just before you get into an 'us-and-them' mentality, please understand that we're all obsessional to some degree. We have to be. Obsessionality is like, say, narcissism and paranoia: you have to have just the right amount of it. If you're too narcissistic you're an arrogant pain in the bum. If not, you don't value yourself enough. If you're too paranoid you can't trust anyone. If not, you're a sucker. Similarly, if you're too obsessional you lose the Big Picture in all the fine detail. If you're not obsessional enough you're so disorganised you'll go nowhere in life. It's all a matter of degree.

■ Now here's a scary thought: we get more obsessional as we get older. That's why old people drive around in old cars. It's not because they can't afford a new car; it's because they can't be bothered learning what all the knobs and gadgets do in a new one. And this trend towards greater obsessionality and lesser flexibility starts in midlife. Beware the creeping tide of rigidity. Keep your gray matter sparking with new ideas and exploration. Once obsessionality sets in you're not young any more ...

GRIEF

If you've escaped any sense of loss in your formative years you surely can't get through midlife without encountering true grief. You've probably already had a taste of it in younger life when you endured all the heartbreaks and rejections of your crushes and passions. But they lasted only days or weeks. True grief lasts months and sometimes years. True grief, like watching loved ones breathe their last and then laying their bodies in the ground, is something we usually first encounter in midlife. So forearm yourself with the following description.

Case history

Eric's wife Eleanor had been feeling vaguely unwell for some weeks. Nothing specific, just fatigue and an ominous malaise. The 'flu, perhaps. Or a mild recurrence of the glandular fever she'd had when she was a teenager. That's what it felt like. A pervasive feeling of illness, and grumpiness to match. After weeks of this Eric's patience ran low and he became snappy towards her. He felt this had all gone on too long and was becoming Eleanor's exercise in self-pity. But the paleness of her face worried him.

Eleanor, always the lady, became distressed when the burps arrived. She couldn't avoid the embarrassing eruptions of air from her swollen stomach. She felt even more tired than before and retired to bed. By now she was having difficulty eating or drinking anything. When the vomiting started she surrendered her refusal to see the doctor.

In the dying remnant of an ancient medical tradition, her G.P. did a housecall. A quick history and physical examination. A frown. 'Your bowel's obstructing. You'll have to go to hospital for some tests.'

Tests? Tests? Her voice had a quaver of fear. It was not unfounded. The following Tuesday a surgeon poked a tube into her anaesthetised abdomen and for the first time her cancer greeted the light of the external world. It was everywhere. Sew her up. Load her up with morphine. Call the padre. She's on her way out.

In the post-operative recovery room she knew the news even before it became words. The surgeon wore the same frown as her G.P.

The padre was a well-intentioned idiot. She said her own prayers. A gray-haired nurse on the ward gave her the best advice she could have hoped for in the circumstances. 'Say your goodbyes to your family before the morphine makes you too dopey. It'll be too late to say anything much by then.' She squeezed the nurse's hand. Woman to woman. Wife to wife. Mother to mother. Three days later, having embraced Eric and their children, she died as the first rays of the morning sun climbed over the horizon. It was all so sudden.

Eric was stunned. For a while he cursed himself for having been unkind to her. He wondered how he could have been so callous as to take her for granted. She'd always been there. But now she was gone. He felt numbed, bewildered, panicked. Where had this awful loss come from? Why? How could he make sense of it?

He had an Eleanor-shaped hole in his life. He'd never felt so alone. At night he'd wake to find himself reaching out for her. He wanted the funeral and wake to be over. He appreciated the well-wishers and visitors but no one could ease his loneliness. He might as well be alone. Forever.

After a few weeks of feeling stunned he broke down. Waves of sadness washed over him. Sometimes anger too. Rage. Who had taken her from him? He railed at God, fate, nature, destiny. And the cancer.

He was quite sure he'd never recover. This was his lot in life: to grieve for Eleanor forever. Just waiting for his own time to come so he could join her. He began formulating how he'd apologise to her in an afterlife they'd share forever.

But just as our wounds heal, so does grief. The reparative process that heals a cut in the skin has a mental equivalent. For Eric it took a year. He could almost mark the hour his mind turned from the past to the future. It coincided with the arrival of springtime and green shoots on the maple tree outside his window. Signs of new life and, for Eric, some greater sense of resignation and optimism. Perhaps he truly could forge a future in a world without Eleanor. Perhaps, just perhaps, he might be able to love someone else as he'd loved her.

There it is. A slightly sanitised history of a natural grief process. Believe it or not, this painful passion that rocks your whole world view to its foundations is actually, for the most part, a predictable process. It can almost be graphed. There's a beginning, a middle and an end.

- In the first phase is the stunned, overwhelmed feeling. It's all too much to take in. Even if someone's death is expected you can never quite prepare yourself for the last breath. Death, after all, is so final. Irreversible. You feel so many feelings so deeply that you just end up feeling numb.

- In the middle phase the emotions burst like a bombed dam. Waves of sadness. Waves of anger. A deep sense of aloneness. A part of you has been amputated. Heartache. A need to understand, to find a meaning, to make sense of this pain. A need to blame, to rant against someone. Or God.

- The final phase is some sort of resolution. Not that you ever really get over it. You just 'come to terms with it', as they say. In some way it never quite goes away. Even if Eric remarried and lived to a ripe old age, memories of losing Eleanor would always invoke sadness.

Keep in mind that we'll all endure grief regularly in our lives. Loss is inevitable. Not just of people, but of our youthful agility, our naïvety, our friends, parents, careers, health. Eventually we lose our own lives. We can't escape grief. When we use mental tricks of denial or repression all we're doing is saving it up so it can visit us again at some stage in the future.

There's a gentle Buddhist parable that comes to mind. Gautama, an Indian prince who is revered as the original Buddha, was approached by a distressed woman whose child had died. He told her he could help her if she could bring him a mustard seed from a household in which no one had died. She hurried away to perform the task, only to discover its impossibility. What household has never encountered death?

DEPRESSION

Don't put your hankies away just yet. Now that you're in a sombre mood I might as well press on with yet another dark pain: depression. Skip this section at your peril. It's rare for me to encounter people who have no idea what this feeling is (although, much to my surprise, they actually do exist). At least one person in five is going to end up with a depression of clinical intensity (i.e. an *illness*, not just a mood) but most of them will either be unaware that their suffering can be eased or struggle on. Waiting. Hoping they'll feel better soon.

It's been often claimed that women experience depression more than men. But that stands in contrast to the statistics, which indicate that men commit suicide four times more often than women. Perhaps men just live in greater states of denial about their emotional states. Or 'medicate' them with alcohol.

Depression, the cruellest of illnesses, often becomes evident in midlife. Probably because of the significant emotional challenges of this stage of our lives. So how does it strike? How will you know if it descends upon you? When does depression as a mood become depression as an illness?

Case history

Charlotte was in her thirties before the first cold wind of gloom crept up on her. She didn't see it coming. It was like watching a plant grow. One of those slow, insidious ones. Dangerous, like Eleanor's cancer. By the time you know it's there, it's everywhere in your life.

The first sign was her lethargy. No interest, no enjoyment, no enthusiasm. Certainly, a little break would occur in her melancholy from time to time. Getting lost in a good movie. Drinking wine and gossiping with friends. But the pall was there most of the time. Little tears would creep from her eyes at the most inopportune time. Like on the bus. Or watching the television news. After all, it's mostly bad news. Her heart ached for everyone in the world who was being bombed or starved. She told herself to buck herself up. Sure, she was down in the mouth but she still had a roof over her head.

Then it began to spill over into her health. She lost her appetite and her clothes became baggy. She found it hard to sleep. In particular she would wake too early in the morning. When she struggled from bed in the morning she was in her blackest mood. She felt she'd slept for five minutes and it took all her fortitude to make herself get under the shower. Sometimes her melancholy would get the better of her and she'd slip between the bedsheets and try to hide there for most of the day.

At a friend's instigation she saw a counsellor. Charming woman, very bubbly and confident. Ruthlessly cheerful. But all Charlotte could do was weep. Talking about her misery didn't seem to help. This wasn't a whistle-a-happy-tune depression. This was a bottle full of pills washed down by brandy sort of depression. She found her thoughts increasingly seeing death as her only escape. One day she did the pills and brandy trick, hoping to never see another wretched day. What she had underestimated was just how difficult it is to kill yourself. Most medications are relatively safe in overdose. You really have to be a pharmacist to know the truly lethal ones. Charlotte underwent the indignity of having her stomach pumped out in the Casualty Department of the nearest hospital. That day, in her hospital gown beneath fluorescent lights in a room that smelled of disinfectant, she met her very first psychiatrist.

Bread and butter stuff. For respiratory physicians it's asthma. For gynaecologists it's period pain. For cosmetic surgeons it's breast implants. For psychiatrists it's depression. Why, oh why, would anyone want to be a psychiatrist? Because watching someone recover from a depression is the most satisfying thing any doctor can experience. It's only after patients respond to treatment that they get a perspective on how depressed they've been. In fact they say the same three things. I've heard them so often I wait for their utterance. They say:

1. I didn't realise how depressed I was.

2. I didn't realise how long I'd been depressed.

3. How could I have thought so negatively?

When they recover they feel like a soldier who's come back from the war. They've been to an awful place, a living hell. They feel alone and traumatised. Worst of all, they can't find the words to adequately describe it to someone. Unless you've been there or witnessed it first hand you can have little concept of what this hideous illness is. And it's dangerous: it kills people.

So do you know whether you're suffering from clinical depression? Or whether you've suffered it in the past? Here's a simple checklist of questions. Keep in mind that you don't have to answer 'yes' to all of these questions, just to most of them. Also, you don't have to experience all these symptoms all the time, *just most of the time, most days.*

■ Do you feel down, sad, flat, gloomy?

■ Is it difficult to take an interest in things, the sort of things that would previously captivate your interest?

■ Is it difficult to enjoy things or to derive pleasure? Like your favourite food, your favourite television programme, a good drop of red wine, etc.

■ Is it difficult to motivate yourself and feel enthusiastic?

■ Has your sex drive diminished? Is 'libido' the capital of Portugal?

■ Do you regularly beat yourself up with messages of guilt, shame, failure?

■ Are you disillusioned (there's that word again) with your life and the world in general? Are you uncharacteristically critical or negative?

- Do you despair for the future?

- Has your sleep pattern changed? Some depressed people sleep too little, others too much. Even those who sleep excessively find that sleep doesn't refresh them. Also, early morning wakening is a cardinal sign of depression. As a rule of thumb, anxious people have trouble getting off to sleep and depressed people have difficulty staying asleep.

- Have you lost your appetite? How much weight have you lost recently? Some depressed people eat more and put weight on, but they're often habitual 'comfort eaters'.

- Does your mood vary during the day? In particular, do you feel worse in the morning and find that your mood warms up during the day? Some depressed people notice this distinct daily change. It's called the *diurnal mood variation*. It screams alarm bells. Another cardinal sign.

- Do you find yourself contemplating suicide? That's the first step. Step two is to think about how you'd do it. Step three is to prepare for it and you know what step four is. If the answer to this question is 'yes', then understand this: you're depressed. You're dangerously depressed. You need treatment, pronto. Skip the counsellor stage. Put this book down and go straight to your doctor.

Enough already with the gloomy stuff. Let's move to another emotional pain: anxiety. The symptoms of anxiety disorders often overlap with those of depression. Sometimes it's hard to know which is the chicken and which is the egg. My advice: leave the intricacies of diagnosis to the experts.

ANXIETY

Once again, I'm harping on because problems with anxiety are common, under-diagnosed and under-treated.

Consider this

You worry too much. You're a tense person. People around you absorb your anxiety. It's hard to be relaxed within your environs. It's like trying to sleep through an air raid.

You seem so irritable. Your frustration tolerance approaches zero. Little problems become magnified.

Diagnosis: Generalised Anxiety Disorder, as described in Chapter 3. Arguably the most common psychiatric disorder of all.

Now consider this

You hate flying. You'd rather be bled by a hundred leeches than step inside an aeroplane. Every time the cabin crew close that door with the big steel handle you feel your heart rate treble and begin to suffocate. You tremble. You sweat. Your mouth goes dry and your bowels turn to water. You get one of those chest pains you've deserved for years and you're sure you must be having a heart attack. A tightness in your throat feels as if your windpipe is closing. You feel faint. If you hadn't been in this situation a dozen times before you'd swear you were dying. But you know exactly what this is. You've been here before. You're in the middle of a blinding panic attack. You fumble for the valium you always carry onto aeroplanes. If this pilot doesn't get this aeroplane onto the ground within the next few minutes you're going to lunge at the big steel handle and let yourself out.

The essence of the panic attack is just that: panic. But the panic can be camouflaged by the plethora of bodily symptoms. People enduring their first panic attack can often be quite convinced they're having a heart attack. They're often carted off to Casualty Departments and hooked up to every piece of electronic technology only to find that their heart is as robust as an athlete's. So later that day they meet their very first psychiatrist.

If you get enough panic attacks it's hard to escape its allied condition: agoraphobia. That's a fear of being in a place from which you can't escape. The usual places, apart from the confines of an aeroplane, are lifts, tunnels, bridges, traffic jams, public transport, wide-open spaces and crowds. If these symptoms ring a bell with you, trot off and see a shrink.

Now consider this

You're more than shy. In fact you're crippled by your shyness. Your phobic stimulus isn't aeroplane doors closing, it's being looked at. Scrutinised. Judged. At the root of this is your fear of losing control, making a fool of yourself, being humiliated. Public speaking is scary for eighty or ninety per cent of the population, but for you it induces all the bodily symptoms of panic.

Diagnosis: social phobia. The most hellish experiences, apart from public speaking, are talking on the telephone, signing your name in front of someone and, for men, peeing in a public urinal – but when you think about it, that's when we men feel most exposed anyway! In most social situations you become preoccupied with whether people can see you blush, see you perspire or hear you stutter. Sounds familiar? If so, you might also be diagnosable with the more pervasive form of social phobia, which is the avoidant personality. It's characterised by not only social anxiety, but also feelings of inferiority or incompetence and an over-sensitivity to criticism or negative evaluation.

We all know people like this. They're usually blissfully unaware that their shyness isn't just shyness: it's a diagnosable disorder. They can actually be helped immensely by group cognitive-behavioural therapy. I won't even begin to try to explain what that means. You'll just have to take my word for it. Or go ask that nice doctor you found when you moved into the district.

Now consider this

You're a shop assistant. You're the epitome of efficiency. Courteous. Slick with the soft-sell. A dab hand with gift-wrapping and the credit-card machine. You take a pride in your work and so you should. You're a first-class shop assistant.

Then one day, when you're alone in the shop a man walks in. As he enters he pulls the 'beanie' hat on his head down and you realise for the first time it's a balaclava. Immediately you know what he's doing and why. When he approaches you behind the counter all you can see is his eyes. They look cruel. He produces a long, sharp knife and brandishes it in your direction. His eyes tell you you'd better do exactly what he says. The man with the cruel eyes needs only one excuse to cut your fingers off. 'Open the till,' he says. You obey. It's all over in a minute or two. Then you're alone. Numbed, like Eric's grief. Standing there feeling like a fool with an empty cash drawer in front of you. You don't know quite what you're supposed to do next. So you burst into tears. And sob and sob and sob.

A few days after this awful trauma you wake screaming in the night. You've had a nightmare in which a man with cruel eyes has stabbed you and your bloody entrails have spilled out into your hands. The nightmares come and go, all with similar themes. You experience 'flashbacks' of the robbery. You become tense, irritable. You startle easily. You seem to be waiting for the next danger, the next assailant, the next horror.

Diagnosis: Post-traumatic stress disorder. Initiated by experiences of helpless horror. Then it haunts you. You'll do anything to avoid re-living it, including 'forgetting' large parts of the trauma. A lot of the time you just live in that same numb feeling you experienced as the trauma acted itself out before your very eyes. The rest of the time you're tense, irritable, anxious.

Get thee to a shrink.

Now consider this

You've lived with them for years. When they first arrived you thought you were going mad. Sometimes they're torturous thoughts and at other times disturbing images. Sometimes they're an overwhelming impulse to do something nasty or stupid. Like punch your friend in the mouth or shout out obscenities in a cinema. They're called obsessions and they're recurring, intrusive, unwanted and tormenting. You wish you could get these thoughts and images out of your mind, but they just keep coming to plague you. They have horrible themes like sex, incest, paedophilia, violence, blasphemy, dirt, disease, bacteria.

Sometimes you find you can 'neutralise' the obsessions by

doing something. Like counting things compulsively. Touching things in a ritualistic way. Washing your hands in Lady Macbeth style, trying in vain to rid yourself of these infernal germs.

In its simplest form the thoughts are called 'obsessions' and the actions are called 'compulsions'. Hence the name: obsessive-compulsive disorder, or O.C.D. for short. This is not a personality trait of obsessionality, as described above. This is a recurring, episodic anxiety disorder. It affects one person in forty and most people *live with it for years and years* before they find out it can even be treated. Don't fall into that trap. Off to the psychiatrist with you!

∞ ∞ ∞ ∞ ∞ ∞ ∞ ∞ ∞ ∞ ∞

So these are the common anxiety disorders. Be aware that if you identify with any of these descriptions you'll also be prone to three complicating factors, namely:

■ Other anxiety disorders. They occur in 'clusters'. If you've got an anxiety disorder you usually have more than one.

■ Depression. If you're anxious enough for long enough you'll get depressed. On the other hand, some people slip into clinical depression and this brings out all their anxiety symptoms: agitation, panic attacks, obsessions, you name it. Chicken and egg stuff.

■ Abuse of sedative medications (like valium) or alcohol. Which leads rather nicely into the next section ...

ALCOHOL

Midlife is when it creeps up on you. You started tippling in your teenage years, usually with some disastrous binge as your debut to the world of grog. Then you got into the habit in your twenties of going to the pub on Friday and Saturday nights. You didn't realise what a bad case of social phobia you had until you admitted just how much you needed this 'Dutch courage'. And anyway the M.O.T.O.S.'s at the pub always looked cuter when you were a bit plastered. Your early sexual experiences were helped along by this great aphrodisiac, although a couple of times you woke in the morning next to someone and couldn't recall who the person was or how you'd got there.

If alcohol was a social and sexual lubricant, it also showed you its harsh side. Your first experiences of violence and car accidents were helped along by the dark angel of ethanol. But that didn't stop you. The dark angel had her claws into you by then.

In midlife, your alcohol consumption has quietly and surreptitiously increased over the years. It's not just weekends now. It's weekends and weekdays and public holidays. It's Lent and Yom Kippur. It's 366 days in leap years. Alcohol is firmly ensconced as part of your life.

So when is a lot of alcohol too much? Venerable bodies of learned doctors have published a variety of definitions of alcoholism. I have a very simple one: it has only three factors. You're running into trouble with alcohol if:

1. *You drink too much.* If a standard drink is one nip of spirits, one glass of wine or a mid-sized glass of beer (equals ten

grams of pure alcohol) then no man is supposed to drink more than four drinks per day and no woman is allowed more than two. Yes, that sounds sexist, but I didn't make up the rules, I promise! Also, there's a catch. You should have at least two alcohol-free days per week. Alcohol shouldn't be part of your routine. It has to be, in some way, special.

2. *You get into trouble.* Legal trouble, relationship trouble, money trouble, health trouble. Pour grog on the ground, and, there, problems will grow.

3. *You can't control it.* I've had countless patients over the years take my message about their excessive alcohol consumption and reassure me, with all earnestness, that they agree they've been hitting the bottle but now they'll bring it into control. Before they leave my consulting room, however, I give them the real challenge: I'll be impressed at their level of control if they can work within the above guidelines, but not for six days or six weeks. Anyone can do that. They have to show to themselves and to me that they can control their alcohol consumption for *six months*. And even then they're not out of the forest. They can never become complacent. Folk who attend Alcoholics Anonymous have a little saying: 'the price of our sobriety is constant vigilance'.

Do you satisfy the three criteria above? Don't even dream you can solve this problem by yourself. You need help. A sober old age is better than no old age at all.

CHAPTER 7

RELATIONSHIPS

Now that you're healthy in body and mind, let's get on with the next aspect of your life that'll need a tune-up in midlife: your relationships. Not just that affair you're having or how you get on with your neighbours, but how you get on with all of the important people in your life. And how it all gets changed in midlife.

MARRIAGE

The honeymoon's over. In fact it ended a decade or two ago. The cold, clammy hand of reality is upon you. And your spouse. By now you know all each other's warts and foibles. Your profligate ways with money. His stinginess. Those revolting sounds your bowel makes. Those revolting sounds his bowel makes too. Not to mention the methane. His raging libido and your failing hormones. Your yearning for romance and erotic excitement. His belief that romance are people who live in Rome.

I expect that discussing marriage in midlife should be one of the biggest sections in this book, but I'm going to gloss over it in a few paragraphs. There are just so many of those books about relationships on the market that go on and bloody on about marriage that I'm bored to tears with it all. I can sum up their message in a sentence. In midlife, marriage is about compromise, tolerance and mutual acceptance; communication (even when it feels like ulcers on your tongue and earache at the same time); handling life's dramas and disappointments; learning about the three F's (fighting, forgiving and making love); and maintaining some passion in the bedroom. There, now all you have to do is get on with it.

I suppose that this sounds like a lot of hard work. In the early stages of your relationship you can live in that la-la land that's called 'falling in love'. As we in the middle years know, that's just nature's cruel little trick to make sure we get each other into the bedroom for hours of carefree bonking. Falling in love is an almost psychotic experience of self-induced delusion, fanned by the ardour of the Loved One, in which we can fantasise about having found The Perfect Person. Then comes the harsh reality. If you skipped the section earlier in this book about disillusionment, you'd better go back and read it about ten times. Starting relationships is easy. Keeping them going is the hard bit.

But just before you find a good divorce lawyer (as if there *are* any!), here's the good news. A wonderful thing happens to marriages in midlife: they get richer. Imagine that!

You see, if someone can tolerate your expanding girth and your methane and still love you, that must be a very strong love, mustn't it? If someone can read your bank statements without packing bags and fleeing to a tax haven, you must be onto a good thing, mustn't you? If you can understand that to have a blazing row doesn't mean you've stopped loving each other, then your love must be rich and deep and mature. Not the silly, exhilarating fantasy of young love. This is The Real Thing.

Perhaps one of the strategies here is to hang onto your

memories of falling in love. Treasure them. Rekindle them regularly. Do little romantic things for each other that indicate you're thinking of this other person. Go on dirty weekends. Hang from chandeliers. Share a banana daiquiri around a swimming pool. Pretend you're young again, even if it's for forty-eight hour stretches. Prove to each other and the world that you don't need youth, stupidity and a copy of the Karma Sutra to be truly in love.

And that brings me onto the next subject ...

SEX

Funny thing, this. If you're to believe Hollywood and the media, sexual intercourse is something that occurs between supermodels and muscular men who look as if they've just come out of a gay calendar. Ever seen a fifty-something striptease artist? Ever seen a blue movie that features octogenarians? Ever seen a woman on hormone replacement therapy leave a lingerie shop chuckling with delight about her latest purchase?

So what about us midlifers? Do balding, overweight, peri-menopausal people with gout have sex too? Of course we do. And what's more (and don't tell the younger generation this – they'll find out when their time comes), red wine isn't the only thing that gets better with age ...

How did we get into this societal self-deception? Kids blanch and go 'yuk' at the concept of anyone over thirty doing The Deed. We all buy into it. Doubt my word? Okay, just try imagining your own parents making love. See?

The hidden reality here is that in midlife there are a number of great things that happen to a sexual relationship. Here are three of them:

1. We men become (slightly) less preoccupied with sexual fantasy. Or, conversely, we grow out of that rather tormented stage of youth in which the only topic of daydreams is doing something lurid with whoever is the film star of our fancy. Now I know that this is a gross generalisation and I'm all too aware that young women can have a libido that over-rides the rational parts of their brains too, but young men swim in a sea of sexual fantasy 'twenty-four-seven'. Time and maturity, as well as dicky testosterone levels (is 'dicky' the right adjective here? ...) mean that our gray matter becomes (slightly) more controlling than our genitalia.

   In previous years we made love as if we'd just been given the ten-minute warning of impending nuclear annihilation; now we know how to linger over lovemaking just as we know how to savour good food. Orgasm is reserved for towards the end of the main course rather than when the entrée hits the table. Dessert becomes a loving and mutually-satisfied cuddle in the aftermath, rather than a hurried re-clothing manoeuvre before someone's parents come home.

   Have you ever wondered about those gorgeous young things who hang around with older partners, both male and female. And you thought they were in it for the money?!

2. We grow more accepting of our less-than-perfect body image. Indeed, as we shall see later in this book, we know

we're coming to the end of midlife when we don't particularly care what other people think of our bodies. And let's face it, only a very small percentage of the population really does look like the supermodel or the guy from the gay calendar. Especially when their age can be measured in scores rather than dozens. The rest of us don't have either the time or the narcissism to hang around in gyms. We've got mortgages to pay and kids to feed. In midlife we become more prepared to use what we have rather than what the fashion magazines say we should have. You know you're really emerging from midlife when you can make love under fluorescent lighting and still have a rollicking good time ...

There's a related phenomenon that emerges in midlife: we often find the goddess (or god) within. That's a quaint New-Agey concept that we ageing hippies use. It's a metaphor for unbridled, confident expression of lust. You can really only achieve this in midlife, because before that you're too worried about your pimples or how you look in photos in the school magazine. You can't see that you're really very attractive because you still think you should look like a supermodel or a gay pin-up. In midlife you can own up to your libido and by now you're also finding out how to express it with a maximum of satisfaction and a minimum of blushing. So here's another of life's little secrets, revealed at last: midlifers do the best bonking ...

3. We discover different forms of sexual intimacy. If you think that sex is all about one type of genitalia engaging the other

type in some horizontal folk dancing, you've got a lot to learn. That's what teenagers believe when they find they have some darkness, the back seat of a car and not a lot of time on their hands. Midlifers, on the other hand, come to realise that sexual intercourse in the evening can begin with a caress in the morning and then build all day to its nocturnal conclusion. Sexual expression isn't just humpy-rumpy, it's every mental, emotional insinuation of seduction. It's what you do with your hands and mouth (upon which I shall not elaborate for fear of alarming anyone aged under thirty-five) and occasionally it's more quick and no-frills than end-of-main-course and satin sheets. Sex can occur over the telephone or even in a letter. It must involve the sharing of sexual fantasies and acting them out. When midlifers say 'I'm all tied up' they're usually speaking from the telephone in their bedrooms.

We midlifers also learn that routine and monotony are the biggest passion-killers. Ours is a time of creativity. If it feels good (and it's not going to get you arrested), do it!

Finally, a cautionary note: if your sex life is failing (or long since dead, buried and pushing up daisies), your marriage is in major trouble. Sex is a barometer of your relationship. Sure, we all go through the good times and the bad times, but sex is the icing on the cake of your relationship. An icing-less cake is edible but not too exciting. We all fall into some regular pattern of sexual expression within our relationships in terms of frequency, nature, number of chandeliers and patterns of stains left on the satin sheets. If the frequency, etc., of your relationship equals zero, you've got a big problem. The barometer is reading 'storm' because it's hard to do horizontal folk-dancing with someone you can't stand. Do something about it before your partner starts looking for one of those 'good' divorce lawyers ...

And now, if we're talking sex, let's mention the natural outcome: kids. They're so much in the hearts and minds of us midlifers that I've devoted the next chapter to them. But first some thoughts on what to do with that *other* generation: your parents.

PARENTS

Why do we live so long these days? A newborn might soon have a life expectancy touching a hundred years. The population pyramid is becoming top-heavy and we midlifers, part of the baby boom, are going to stretch that pyramid even further in only a few years' time. Sociologists and evolutionists hypothesise that old folk play an important purpose in society: with the passing of the hunter-gatherer and carer-nurturer roles and both parents working these days, the older generation is supposed to be helping anyone younger. Fountains of inheritance and grandparental baby-sitters 'on tap'. That's the theory, but the booming trend to make oldies huddle together in retirement villages does rather contradict that notion. So what are you, as a midlifer, planning to do with *your* parents?

Exercise

1. If your parents are still alive, go and visit them.

2. Look deeply into their eyes and at their faces.

3. There, you're looking at your future. I hope you like what you see ...

Shakespeare summed it up in his sonnet about the seven ages of man. We begin life bald and toothless and end up 'sans eyes, sans hair, sans teeth, sans anything'. Francophobes should be aware that 'sans' means 'without'. The Buddhists are right when they speak of the *impermanence* of everything. I suppose the only consolation for the problem of ageing is that it happens slowly and, hopefully, gracefully.

And how do you handle it when your parents die? Scan Chapter 6 again for the section on grief. Or perhaps own up to less grief and more relief, depending upon the quality of the relationship you shared with them. From a practical point of view you might need to think about two things:

■ It's important to try to heal old wounds (we all have them) before your parents die. Now the elderly usually become less able to cope with new notions of breaking out of their beloved routine – that's why they don't have e-mail addresses – so don't be surprised if you try to get close to distant parents but find they still reject you. Be that as it may, you might get lucky and find that they still have the resources and, paradoxically, the maturity to listen to you and use whatever time they have left to repair the damage in your relationship. The object of the exercise is to do what you can when they're still around. Or, conversely, to avoid burying them with the nagging idea that you should've tried to get closer. Because by then, needless to say, it's too late.

■ If you're going to embark upon this one-last-chance scheme, do it sooner rather than later. If your parents go demented (i.e. sans marbles as well as their teeth and hair) they'll usually do that quite slowly, so don't miss the opportunity when it's there. Also, if your parents are dying, especially of cancer, they'll usually get loaded up with narcotics, such as morphine, toward the end. At that point the only communication you'll manage with them will be with picture cards, so it'll be another lost opportunity.

Now consider this

I buried my father. Literally. After his coffin was laid in the ground my family and I picked up shovels and filled in the grave. I understand this might be an Irish tradition but for us it came more from Maori mores. We didn't want strangers to complete such an emotionally important task. Now I've instructed my own children that I don't want them to walk away from my own grave without repeating this very meaningful gesture.

After we'd finished I was standing at the graveside with one of my brothers, both of us leaning on shovels. He turned to me and said 'Get the feeling we're next?'

So life goes on. When you're 'next' it gets you thinking about all sorts of morbid things to do with mortality. I'll come back to those topics in future chapters.

INFERTILITY

It's so simple. You find a partner. Then, when the time is opportune (and not a moment earlier) you start 'trying' for a family with your partner. (For 'trying' read 'bonking' ... never have I encountered a sillier euphemism). Then you make babies. Then, when you're over the baby thing (you just *know* when that is), you stop making them and wait a few decades to become a grandparent. Now what could be less complicated than that?

There are two groups of people who deviate from this neat plan. First there are the people who bonk but are not 'trying'. They just get unlucky when some stubborn embryo reminds them of their utter incompetence in the field of contraception (see above). Then there are the people who are 'trying' but can't create any embryos ... or at least none stubborn enough to hang around.

So consider this scary statistic: one in seven couples has problems with fertility. And that doesn't count the people who are fertile, but childless. They just can't find anyone with whom they'd like to make babies. For a lot of people it's just not that simple after all. The interesting thing is that very few of us really stop to consider the possibility that we may be unable to breed. Infertility is a nasty hunch that begins to dawn on us after about a year of unproductive 'trying'.

So what happens to these poor unfortunates? They go through hell, that's what happens. They get trotted around a lot of doctors. They undergo investigations and procedures that need not be recorded here because some kids might get hold of this book and be indelibly traumatised by the descriptions. The poor unfortunates get plenty of their own trauma. As well as sorrow, aloneness, misunderstanding and an inexorable frustration that never quite goes away. The list of emotional consequences of infertility goes something like this:

- *Disillusionment.* Go back and read Chapter 3. Disillusionment is the constellation of feelings induced by the loss of a pleasurable fantasy. The fantasy here, shared by all who 'try', is that an embryo will result, prove its stubbornness and then induce several hours of excruciating labour pain before emerging as the most beautiful baby the world has ever welcomed. Then, after a few years, during which The Stubborn One's mother will mysteriously 'forget' how excruciating her labour pains were, along will come the second, and even third, Stubborn One. That's how it's supposed to work. Infertile couples must grapple with the feeling that this quaint image may prove illusory to them.

- *Depression* can be one of the worst consequences. About one-fifth of women undergoing the indignity of 'assisted reproduction' (another absurd euphemism for steel pipes poked into abdomens and people made in glass dishes) will slip into a black hole of sheer, frustrated misery.

- A *sense of failure* is almost inevitable. What's more, this is failure of a deeply personal, private, intimate nature. A failure of masculinity and/or femininity. An inability to achieve what silly teenagers who bonk in cars achieve without even 'trying'.

- To make matters worse, infertile couples are repeatedly confronted by *reminders* of their perceived 'failure'. Family gatherings with well-meaning aunts who ask too many personal questions. Nappy advertisements with cute poo-free babies and soppy jingles. The annual insults of Mothers' Day, Fathers' Day and Christmas. Dinner parties during which everyone talks about their kids. Standing by football fields to watch their nephews play and not their sons. The list goes on.

- *Avoidance.* Surprise, surprise. No wonder infertile couples huddle together in mutual support. No wonder they stop going to the Christmas gatherings of the extended family with all the progeny playing and fighting over gifts and food. That way they can also avoid the ignorant comments that people make when they learn of the infertility. They can get sick of parents saying how lucky they are and joking about giving one of their own kids to the infertile ones.

- *Marginalisation.* No wonder, too, that they feel different in society. Like another race.

- *Amputation.* They feel that some part of them is missing, as if they'd lost a leg in the war. In a way, it is missing. Just as we parents feel our children are a part of us, so do the infertile sense that this part of them is missing. And with it the enjoyment and sense of fulfilment they see in the eyes of parents playing with their kids.

So how do you handle this agony? First, get the best medical advice. See what you can do about it and then do your best to make it work. But if you're going in for all sorts of medical interventions in an attempt to find the stubborn embryo, it's also important to set an 'end-point', i.e. just how many tubes and glass dishes you'll tolerate before you have to give in. I wonder how many 'assisted reproduction' centres publicise their failure rate? Quite a few, I suspect, because most of these interventions fail and have to be tried over and over again. Plan early when you're going to give up so you can try to prepare yourself for the emotions that will flood in ...

If medical interventions are not your cup of tea and it's clear you're going to be childless then you'll probably need some professional help to cope with the disappointment. This will take some time. Like years rather than weeks or months. Be patient. Be honest.

AFFAIRS

How common are affairs? Who knows? When researchers survey this sort of topic, how honest are the responses? Not very, I suspect. So let's just work on the presumption that affairs are pretty common. Now throw in every fling, one-night-stand and drunken mistake and you're starting to get the impression that there's a whole lot of extra-marital bonking going on.

In my work I've encountered so many patients describing the devastating emotional consequences of infidelity that I've come to realise that your 'average' affair (if such a thing exists) is so predictable you can 'plot' it. Affairs run through thirteen-and-a-half phases. I'll try to describe them within the context of an affair between a single woman and a married man. I suspect that this is the most common scenario but, once again, who's to know? Read on.

- Phase one. They meet. There's an initial attraction but she knows he's married. They enjoy some sort of business or social interaction. A bit of flirtation ensues. Both find themselves fantasising about each other.

- Phase two. An 'opportunity' arises. Or is engineered by the sneakier of the two, usually him. It might be that they're away on a conference or he pops in to give her a neighbourly visit. Either way, his wife is definitely not in the vicinity, or in his mind.

- Phase three. They find that not only are they good at flirtation but they're both rather enjoying it. She puts up a token resistance, but by now their hormones have kicked in. The consumption of alcohol always facilitates this phase, which culminates in the first illicit kiss.

- Phase four. This follows very quickly. Sometimes in the time it takes to enter the nearest bedroom. She's busily trying to ignore the alarm bells that are going off in her head and his silky seduction is a great help in doing this. Some passionate, albeit clumsy, love-making follows. Now it's 'on'.

- Phase five. The first turbulence. She, and possibly he, have an attack of guilt. But they keep in contact, long enough for ...

- Phase six. Another couple of bonks. It's still 'on'.

- Phase seven. Her scruples plague her a bit, more so than his do. But the sex is getting better and better. She even finds it convenient when he gets out of bed and goes back to his wife. He's not cluttering up her life. For now, the affair suits them both.

■ Phase eight. Time passes. They get into a routine. As before, the routine is set up to suit him. She's more flexible.

■ Phase nine. She gets restless. By now it doesn't feel good when he goes back to his wife. This affair is set up to suit him, not her. She's learning a sad lesson about bonking: you can't be sexually intimate with someone over a period of time without coming to want and need that person as a regular fixture in your life. Even though we'd like to be promiscuous like the rest of the animal kingdom, human beings need sexual relationships to be exclusive and committed. Damn these emotional complications!

■ Phase ten. She begins to pressure him to leave his wife and be with her. He responds by giving one of the Three Common Excuses:

 – the wife excuse: he can't leave his wife because she'd never cope and she'd commit suicide ...

 – the money excuse: he can't leave his wife because his work or business is not going so well and he can't afford to support his family and her. Not just yet ...

 – the kids excuse: he can't leave his kids because they're too young, or needy, or whatever.

■ Phase eleven. Either way, the affair drags on and on and on. This phase can take years. She feels more resentful and depressed. She threatens to end the affair several times but he seduces her back. Now it's more about dependence than love. The magic is being slowly drained out of their sex life. She feels like a prostitute.

- Phase twelve. She creates a crisis. She usually does this by bluntly or sneakily informing his wife of the affair. She does this because she's quietly desperate. That way he'll have to choose between these two women.

- Phase thirteen. He chooses his wife. She usually takes him back and they stay together, but their marriage is never the same. After all, he's betrayed her once, why shouldn't he betray her again? Every time he's late home from work she panics.

- Phase thirteen-and-a-half. If he does choose his mistress, the chances of that relationship working out is just about zero. He hasn't resolved all the reasons he got into the affair in the first place, the mistress doesn't understand any of the ramifications of being stepmother to his kids and, sooner or later, he's going to dump guilt trips on her about ruining his marriage.

There. The Archetypal Affair. Pardon me if I sound moralistic, but an affair is a situation in which three people end up getting hurt. Think about it.

DIVORCE

When we midlifers were kids, very few couples divorced. When they did, it was something of a scandal. A pall of shame descended onto the couple and, worst of all, on the innocent victims: their kids. The words 'broken marriage' were whispered behind hands with a nod and a wink.

How times have changed. In my adoptive homeland of Australia, 40 per cent of marriages now end in divorce. And the divorce rates increase exponentially with every subsequent marriage. One of my mottoes is that 'one divorce is a tragedy, two divorces is a symptom and three divorces is a diagnosis'. A diagnosis of what? I haven't worked that out just yet but, at the very least, habitual divorcees show some recurring difficulties with either choosing partners or sustaining relationships or, for want of a better word, their 'stickability'.

So why do people resort to divorce? It depends upon when they do it. It strikes me that there are three patterns here: the early divorce, the sudden-later divorce and the gradual-later divorce. Midlifers should take particular note of the latter two, because if your own marriage hasn't had a brush with these problems you'll undoubtedly witness them in your contemporaries. To elaborate:

■ The early divorce is when the marriage falls apart within the first few years. It's the most common pattern and usually precipitated by people realising they shouldn't have got married in the first place. Sometimes, early divorcers were in a rush to leave an oppressive home environment and getting married was the only way to escape. Sometimes they married out of lust or in a smitten state of blind naïvety. Often, they're young. Usually they weren't engaged for too long. Sometimes one or other of the couple will subsequently admit they had increasing doubts about getting married the closer they came to the wedding date but felt they couldn't pull out because everyone was swept up into the hype of the occasion.

■ The sudden-later divorce occurs when marriages seem to be going swimmingly, superficially at least, when some thunderous trauma, complicated by betrayal, gives the marriage a monumental kick in the guts. The traumas usually involve either sex or money, i.e. the revelation of an affair, compulsive gambling or loss of control of a drug or alcohol habit. Midlifers beware: your impending midlife crisis can also serve as the 'kick', particularly if you get an overwhelming urge to wear saffron robes and renounce pleasures of the flesh.

- The gradual-later divorce happens when marriages die slowly. The couple report that they 'drifted apart'. Stresses like money problems, unemployment, delinquent kids and changing values in midlife can accentuate the 'rot'. As always, your sexual relationship is the barometer of your marriage so, if your marriage has been a bonk-free zone for several years you might be witnessing the slow death of your marriage. Be aware, too, that marriages run in five to nine year cycles of togetherness versus apartness, hence the so-called 'seven-year itch'. Every five to nine years, couples usually find they're drifting apart in terms of their interests, values, personal development, etc. They hit a crisis point, when they must either bring their relationship together or break it up. This is where the 'stickability' factor comes in. If you want to make it work, you have to do the work.

So, let us presume that the scales have fallen from your eyes and you realise you have to end your marriage. How do you do it? I reckon there are four Golden Rules:

1. There has to be an end-point. Nothing is more emotionally confusing than when couples come and go, the relationship being on-again, off-again. With marriage it takes two to Make

it and one to Break it. The Breaker has to be honest and have the courage to see it through.

2. Communication has to be unambiguous. The most common mistake I observe is that Breakers know they are hurting their partner, so they try to water down their harsh messages. Rather than saying the marriage is over, they talk about 'trial separations'. Rather than saying 'I don't love you anymore', they say 'I love you but I have to leave you'. The other party only hears the 'I love you' bit and ignores the second half of the sentence. The result of this well-intentioned ambiguity is that the pain becomes worse, not better.

3. When a couple splits up, the best thing they can do is to get out of each other's lives. Don't fantasise you can turn a loving relationship into a friendship. Or at least not overnight.

4. Don't triangulate the kids. When a couple splits up, they often adopt a 'you're for me or against me' sort of paranoid stance. They try to drag friends and family into this triangulation too. But the greatest victims are the children. They can have all sorts of destructive roles foisted upon them: the mediator, the scapegoat, the trophy, the counsellor, the champion, the punching-bag, the message-bearer, etc. For your kids' sake, keep them out of the triangle.

So what happens *aprés* divorce? Divorcees usually go through a number of phases after the separation. First, there might be a honeymoon phase, particularly for the Breaker, in which there is a wonderful sense of lightness and freedom. Then the realities of having to adjust to the singles scene again emerge. Men often jump straight into what has come to be called the 'transitional relationship', i.e. they try to bed the first woman who shows any interest in them. These relationships are seldom long-term. Their purpose is to revive a flagging male ego, even if the women involved are unaware of the game in which they're involved.

Remember that men are far more dependent than women: two-thirds of divorces are initiated by the wife and divorced men stay single for relatively short periods of time: in fact they seem hell-bent on getting shacked up again as soon as possible.

Women after the 'honeymoon phase' of separation often make a sad discovery: their married friends don't trust them anymore. It's part of the way women can hurt women: groups of married women become threatened by the presence of an 'available' woman in their circle.

So is all the heartache of divorce worth it? With the escalating divorce rate I can't help thinking that people have become too wimpy when it comes to staying and battling through the difficulties of relating. After all, even the best marriage requires constant cultivation and stamina on the part of the cultivators. But then, research into divorced couples reveals an interesting fact: a year or two after divorce 80 per cent of men and 90 per cent of women are pleased to be divorced. Also, in these shameless days, children seem to manage to survive their parents' divorces reasonably well, but never quite unscarred. A lot depends upon how empathically their parents worked through the steps.

So, once again, where does the balance lie?

FRIENDSHIP

Midlifers, one and all, take stock of your friendships. After all, God gave you your friends because your family's such a disaster ...

Unlike acquaintances, good friends are hard to find. In midlife you must be wary of the bad habits that can creep into your friendships: laziness, intolerance, an inability to resolve hurts or grievances. To make it worse, you make your most enduring friendships when you're younger because you're usually single, more receptive to friendly overtures and more needy of companionship. Now you're married and in midlife you're probably more selective – and less flexible – with your friendships. The risk, particularly for men, is that you'll be so selective you'll end up alone.

Keep in mind that friends, like lovers, are people you usually can't go looking for. On the contrary, they usually walk into your life. They're workmates or neighbours or folk from the church. Remember, also, that most of us turn our friends over every ten years or so, even if there are hopefully some enduring friendships within the circle.

People are very idiosyncratic in the structure of their friendships. By this I refer to the observation that some people thrive on one or two close friendships while others need to move in a 'pack'. Most of us strive for the balance of having an inner and outer circle.

The friendship issue is different for both genders. Women make friends more easily. They're not cursed with male paranoia or homophobia. They open their hearts more easily, but in the process they can be hurt. Men, on the other hand, often live behind emotional walls with a moat of suspicion or rivalry and a raised drawbridge. But if they allow friends into their castle, this sort of mateship can be strong and enduring. Having said that, I'm often concerned at meeting midlife men who appear to be friendless. The male curse.

So how do you establish and develop true friendships? It takes sensitivity and hard work, like any relationship. You have to hold out the hand of friendship and accept it graciously when it's offered to you. Then you have to nurture the friendship. I've never seen anyone do it better than my mate Jack.

Case history

Again, this is a true one. Jack's my mate. Jack's good at cultivating friendships. Not only does he have a natural charm, but he's had to hone this skill over the years. Why? Because Jack's an airline pilot.

You and I would look at Jack's job and think it must be very glamorous and exciting. But Jack will tell you the truth. It's boring. Spelt booooring. Endless hours of sitting up the sharp end of the aeroplane with the autopilot on. Jack's only needed if something goes wrong. He looks forward to things going wrong because it gives him something to do. Nothing pleases Jack more than landing the great iron bird in the middle of a storm.

So why's Jack so good at friendship? Because he has to be. He'll spend tonight in London and tomorrow in Shanghai. He's away from home a lot of the time so he's established not a girl but a group of friends in every port. He really works on it. As his suitcase comes off the carousel at the airport he's already on his mobile phone calling up someone. Let's have a drink together after work. Grab your missus and let's all go out to dinner. Jack's a master at it. So could you be if you'd just put in the effort.

CHAPTER 8

KIDS

Question: What's the most expensive thing in the world?
Answer: Free sex.
Conclusion: If you bonk enough and you're not a whizz-kid with contraception you'd better get used to terms like 'trimester' and 'neonatal' and, worst of all, 'nappies'. Also 'child support payments' for those scoundrels who have bonked and run. Children, you see, are expensive creatures, as every sagging, midlife parent will be delighted to tell you again and again.

Let's return, momentarily, to the hippie within all of us midlifers. After all, we're part of the Baby Boom that exploded after the Second World War. I've already made mention of the 1960s. You know, Woodstock, Carnaby Street, free love (ha, ha!), Vietnam and the Cold War (and you thought that referred to a post-argument stand-off) ... But life had been safe and predictable in the post-war era. You knew where you stood, even if you didn't particularly like it. Rebuilding, prosperity, sprawling suburbs to accommodate the outflow from crowded maternity hospitals. A belief in nationalistic ideals, loyalty (even to the point of dying for some flag or other), the institutions of law and the Church. But with it came conformity, intolerance and parochialism. Families, and societies, were run on tight rules, roles and expectations.

Around this time something strange began happening to

society in general and families in particular. There was a rebellious, egocentric entitlement to self-expression. The Me-Generation was well and truly on its way. The Vietnam war was beamed into every Western family's living room and colour television showed us that the blood of the Vietnamese was red too. From then on, the military illusions were shaken. Wars were less about heroism and more about hell. And around this time of extraordinary turmoil we midlifers arrived. In our lives, so far, we've seen these changes:

FAMILY PLANNING

When we were young, people still married young and had heaps of kids. In our lifetimes we have witnessed the arrival of family planning. What a great idea! You can decide when to start having kids, how many to have, spaced at what intervals, and when to dispatch your reproductive abilities to the never-never because it's time to stop procreating. Or at least that's the theory. It's pretty obvious that there are still plenty of people who haven't quite mastered the practice.

So given this supposed element of choice, is it better to have your kids when you're younger (say, twenty-something) or older (say, late thirties)?

- Younger parents have youth, agility and naïvety on their side. It's actually good to be young and stupid when they bring their first baby home. They handle the sleepless nights so much better. They never had much, so the poverty of young parenthood doesn't rob them of previous luxuries. They can even take their kids on the roller-coaster at fun parks and enjoy it as much as the brats do. They also have the pleasure of hanging around in the grandparent/matriarch/patriarch role for an extra decade, much to the consternation of both of the next generations.

But for younger parents, life is an awful struggle unless some recently-deceased rich uncle has left them enough loot to take away the financial strain. What's more, younger parents might one day look back and realise that their childless friends were having a lot more fun with a lot more disposable income than they did at the time.

■ Older parents might have a better idea of what they're letting themselves in for. Or at least they think they do. They read all the pregnancy books and go to ante-natal classes and, poor them, they *believe* all that stuff! They also try to do things just right. They like to be in control of everything. They really think that breathing exercises in labour will give them a drug-free birth (but sometimes they end up screaming in high decibels for drugs, any drugs). Your first baby, like your first parachute jump, is something that shouldn't be too premeditated, otherwise you'll never do it ...

But on the other hand, older first-time parents have life experience (if not wisdom) on their sides. They've frolicked on sandy beaches and dined in restaurants that have had more stars than the Milky Way. All of their rich uncles have long since passed away and the word 'mortgage' is a dewy-eyed memory. So bringing a baby home doesn't mean they have to move to the poor side of town. It does, however, mean that they must confront an uncomfortable, alien feeling: pre-progeny they were in control of their lives. Now everything they do is controlled by, timed around and for the benefit of this *mewler and puker*, to borrow a Shakespearean phrase. Mother has to breastfeed, so the boardroom meeting will simply have to wait ...

And endowed with family planning, how many kids do you *choose* to have? Two-point-zero? Three-point-zero? And when do you know it's time to stop breeding? Answer: you just do, usually. It's like closing a chapter on your life. Somehow your sense of your own identity changes: you *were* a parent of small children, but not *now*. Now you're a parent of school-aged children, the youngest of whom will always be called 'the baby', even when he or she is fifty. Soon you'll be the parent of teenagers and then the heartache starts all over again ...

THE 'GENERATION GAP' (OR LACK OF IT)

In the 1960s there was a lot of talk about the Generation Gap. That's because the Gap was much too big. Short-haired parents were stuck in conservatism and nationalism, glad to be alive in the post-war years. Dreadlocked kids were stuck in pacifist, pot-smoking rebellion confronting the futility of imminent nuclear annihilation. They were like two species, each with a different dialect. No wonder they never got on.

We midlifers, on the other hand, have embraced liberalism as a doctrine. If our kids smoke pot we're so relieved they're not on anything 'harder'. We had to express *amour* in the back seats of cars in the days when parents fantasised we'd stop being virgins when we got married. These days we pay for our daughters' pill prescriptions. We had to be home by midnight. Our kids have to be home by Tuesday. Or Thursday at the latest. If they don't mind.

Now here's a thought: have we gone too far? Can a generation gap be too small? Can parents be too liberal? Too wishy-washy? Too pal-sy? Too reticent to lay down boundaries of decent behaviour? You bet. Boundaries aren't just pointless rules; we tell our kids what to do because we care about them. No boundaries, no care. No boundaries, no mutual respect.

Consider this

You're a schoolteacher. You begin the first day of the school term with all guns blazing. You convince the class that any lapses in discipline will result in an Armageddon of detentions. Then, over the next few weeks you can soften up a bit. From time to time you come down hard if discipline is getting lax. That's how you do it: hard first, then soft. Then hard again from time to time if it's necessary. You know you can't start soft or the kids will walk over you. Worse, the kids will have no *respect* for you. Firm boundaries first, then you can slacken off a bit. So it is that kids, even when they're teenagers, look to parents for some sort of limitation of behaviour. Because then they know where they stand. They feel safe.

Now consider this

Family therapists often classify families on a spectrum which has 'the enmeshed family' up one end and 'the disengaged family' down the other.

Enmeshed Families

These run like autocratic companies. There is strong leadership at the top, but usually strong to the point of being dictatorial. The leader/parent is inherently fragile and must shore up his or her own position of authority by being overly controlling. There's an over-emphasis on rules. When the obsessional leader-parent shows up, everyone ducks for cover. Children/employees of these families/companies run on fear. There's a lot of buck-passing to avoid responsibility.

These families have strong boundaries. It's hard for people to enter or exit them. Even when the kids grow up and marry, their spouses will never really be good enough to belong to The Family. But when kids in these families grow up they usually flee. They get as far away from this control as they can. Enmeshed families 'explode'. Then a sad thing happens. These apostate children have been so controlled for so long they haven't realised that they must now be in control of, and responsible for, their own lives. So, like kids who've left authoritarian schools (and promptly fail their first year at university), or prisoners who are unable to cope with the lack of structure in The Outside World, they go on a sex-and-drugs binge for the next couple of years before they finally grow up. During this binge, they feel wonderfully free but unnervingly out of control.

Enmeshed families have a strong sense of group identity and belonging, but at the expense of individuality, creativity and flexibility. When we midlifers were born, this was how families worked.

Disengaged Families

These have poorer boundaries. People can wander into and out of these families. All the kids might have a different surname. There isn't much of a sense of leadership or rules, but there's a great sense of individuality.

This is how families have evolved in the past few decades. The rules have slackened off. There's an emphasis on individuality and kids are there to be heard as well as seen. Your offspring can make their own mistakes and learn from them. That way they don't have to endure their two-year sex-and-drugs spree when they finally leave home (if they ever do). Or so the theory goes. Anyway, the emphasis is on greater individual identity but at the expense of a sense of belonging. So what's so wrong with that?

Now consider this

You're fourteen. You think you know it all. Or at least you're convinced you know much, much more than your parents. Then there's a major downturn in your life. One day you come home expecting to find your parents in yet another of their interminable arguments. But this day's different: your dad's gone. Had enough. Packed up and moved on. Your mum tells you he's run away with a piece of blonde fluff from his workplace. She's weepy, then angry, then weepy again. After a few weeks, and a couple of brief and highly unsatisfactory telephone conversations with your father, life sort of returns to normal. You don't see much of your dad over the next year and your mum seems to have retreated into her own world. Whatever umbrella of parental control previously existed has just been blown inside out by the cruel winds of divorce. You're your own agent. No one's going to discipline you because they're each wrapped up in their own selfish misery.

You start to skip school. You hang around town with kids who are five years older than you. You learn how to smoke and drink even if it makes you choke or throw up. One of your new 'friends' teaches you the intricacies of shoplifting. Then 'break and enter'. The other kids in your class at school think you're a hero(ine). No dumb parents to tell you what to do. You can do whatever you damned-well like.

But that's the problem. Like kids who escape from the enmeshed family and then don't know what to do with all this freedom, you feel awful. Your schoolmates envy you. So why do you feel so out of control? So bewildered by all this power? So alone? So unloved?

Now consider this

You're a step-parent. You're not Robinson Crusoe here: divorce rates seem to only go upwards. You've coupled up with the love of your life. But he/she comes with three little complications in the form of kids who don't bear any of your genes.

So how do you relate to these step-kids? I've heard a hundred people in this situation say they just want to be their step-children's *friend*. Boy, are they in for a shock! You can't be their friend because they don't want or need you in that role. And you can't be their parent because they've already got two of those. You're not in the kids' generation and you don't have the history or DNA to come anywhere near being a parent. Or at least not overnight.

You're about to find out that being a step-parent is a position for which there is no 'job description'. You're also about to find out that generation gaps and boundaries between adults and children in a family are very necessary for a whole variety of reasons. It's no accident we have government and voters, officers and men, clergy and parishioners, management and staff.

Some boundaries are necessary. One generation earns the money and the next generation spends it. So the saying goes. And so it is with boundaries, discipline and generation gaps. One generation is too controlling and the next too liberal. Sometimes my own kids sound reactionary. Have we midlifers gone too far with our liberalism? This is your life and these are your kids. You be the judge.

GENDER STUFF

One thing our wrinkly old parents had to contend with was the upheaval in gender roles. It started with World War Two when all the menfolk were off fighting whoever was the foe of the day. Women left the hearth behind and toiled in the factories that had previously been a male domain. Then the sixties and beyond: Gloria Steinem, Germaine Greer, etc. Women were 'equal'.

We midlifers have also seen the arrival and departure of waves of gender politics. We've seen men hit their own identity crisis and a tree-hugging, drum-beating men's movement emerge. We've witnessed the invention of the SNAG (Sensitive New Age Guy). And, more recently, we've seen some sort of homeostasis evolve into a comfortable co-existence of genders without the extremist swings of the recent past.

My wife went to university in the late 1990s. For three years she knocked around with a lot of young people. What she found surprised and delighted her. Things were more different than she could ever have imagined. Young women had more confidence and a sense of entitlement. Young men and women interacted with fun and mutual respect rather than shyness or sexual tension.

The waves of change still come and go. But we midlifers are probably more comfortable with our half-blurred gender roles and respect for each other than ever before. And with that comfort has emerged a much greater degree of sexual honesty.

Our parents did It in the dark. We do It on the beach. When we were growing up It wasn't talked about. Now we wish people would just shut up about It. Our parents learned how to do It by lots of trials and lots of errors. We buy the manual, which comes with a rather colourful video. Our childhood was characterised by naïvety. Our children know a lot. Too much, perhaps.

Newton was wrong: for every *action* there's an *over-reaction*.

Now here's a thought: how do you manage it when your own kids become sexually active? How do you react when they start doing exactly what you did (or tried to do) when you were their age? I expect that the biggest challenge is the daddies-and-daughters one, despite all the sexual equality ideals I've just written.

When do we accept the notion that our adolescent kids won't be home tonight because they'll be sleeping with their lover? When are the brat and lover allowed to do It under your own roof? It was so easy for your parents: they just said no, never, not in my house. Not until after the honeymoon. But that confined you to illicit lovemaking in places you'd prefer not to remember. As you can see, I seem to have asked more questions than I've come up with answers ...

We midlifers are surely the first Western generation to be more sexually tolerant. Only a few pre-contraception generations ago premarital sex was associated with not only the risk of incurable venereal disease (how HIV has turned back the clock!) but also the unfortunate possibility that parts of your precious DNA might be scattered to the winds of promiscuity. Worse, that you might have grandchildren you'll never enjoy or even get to know. Sex, after all, is a dangerous game. It's what breeders do.

Some of these horrors have been realised. But the gain has been the abolition of the absurd myth that people don't have a libido until their wedding night. What we have now is more rational. Our children can have a sexuality and a libido, just as we did when we were their age, and they can express it in a constructive way. Now that's what I call progress.

DRUGS

At some stage you've going to find that your kids come home from a party with bloodshot eyes and a benign smile, asking whether there are any leftovers in the fridge. They've been into the dope. Marijuana, hash, pot, grass, weed, whatever it's currently called. Or they won't come home until dawn because they've been dancing all night. Suspect amphetamines ('speed'), cocaine or ecstasy ('MDMA' by its chemical name). If you realise your kids have been wearing a long-sleeved shirt for the last two years (even at the swimming pool) you'd better check out their forearms for needle punctures and 'track marks'. Welcome to midlife.

What would our own parents have done in this situation? They would've freaked right out. They would've told us how marijuana was the thin end of the wedge and that it was only a matter of time before pot-smokers ended up on heroin. They might've dragged us off to a drug rehab centre, believing they were saving our lives. Then they would've gone home to console themselves with their liquor and cigarettes.

Times have changed. We don't believe that all pot-smokers become heroin addicts these days. Anyone in midlife has lived through the 1960s and therefore, *ipso facto*, is a hippie at heart. Also, unlike ex-President Clinton, we *did* inhale, it's just that we don't tell our kids that. Unless we didn't grow out of it and we're inhaling with them. Or they can smell leaves burning from behind our locked bedroom doors at times when they're disappointed we're taking drugs and not having midlife sex.

So what do you do when your kids take drugs? Note the word 'when', not 'if'. Research shows that 70 per cent of adolescents have experimented with drugs. Those researchers must have surveyed kids at the local fundamentalist Christian school. I think the figure is more like 90 per cent. So chances are your own kids are going to dabble, perhaps become 'recreational' users, or perhaps end up in the long-sleeved shirt. Here is a crash-course in what you need to know about the drug scene. And if you're still dabbling with drugs yourself, you'd better read this twice.

■ Work on the presumption that your kids have at least experimented with drugs. If they come unstuck with chemicals, you have to be their biggest resource person.

■ When does 'recreational use' become addiction? When you

lose control of your drug and it causes damage in your life. When you hang out for it and get nasty symptoms if you don't have it. When it becomes a central aspect of your life and your routine. When you make sure you've always got a regular supply of it. When it causes conflict in your relationships or damages your health. When you get arrested (and include drink-driving in that). When your partner, your doctor, your bank manager and your favourite police sergeant tell you to give it up. *That's* when you're addicted. And keep in mind that most addicts live in a state of denial about their addiction.

■ We long ago gave up the quaint notion about drugs being either physically or psychologically addictive, or both. All drugs are both. Even marijuana has a withdrawal syndrome: regular dope-smokers get twitchy if they have a few days 'off'. They become restless, irritable, sleepless and not a lot of fun to be around.

■ Some drugs in some people can induce psychosis. That means they can send the user mad. Bonkers. Insane. There are two magical ingredients. The first is some sort of predisposition to psychosis in the victim. That's probably in your genes, but keep in mind that big doses can send just about anyone into the psychiatric ward. It does mean, however, that drug use can unveil a latent schizophrenia. The drug doesn't cause the psychosis, it just *reveals* it. The second magical ingredient is the type of drug. The ones that are stimulant in any way are the ones that will introduce you to your first psychiatrist. I'm referring to marijuana, amphetamines, ecstasy and cocaine. So how do you know whether any particular drug will drive you mad? Here's the problem: you have to try it to find out.

■ Speaking of heroin, let me remind you of the famous statement of an unknown heroin addict: 'I envy people who've never tried heroin because they don't know how good it is.' Think about it. The intoxicant effects of heroin are very, very pleasant. That's why the stuff is so addictive and so dangerous. Yes, there are recreational heroin users out there, but I suspect that most of them eventually cross that line into addiction. You'll see them at the swimming pool. They're the ones in the long-sleeved shirts.

■ A word on needles. When I was at medical school I recall doing a laboratory exercise in which we had to prick our own fingers with a sterile lancet, squeeze a drop of blood and then look at it under the microscope. I'm pleased to say that I found it physically and mentally impossible to prick myself. But the student next to me took considerable pleasure in digging the lancet into my sweaty digit. If my memory serves me right he went on to become a second-rate surgeon. So why am I telling you this? Because anyone who puts a needle into his or her own arm is, by definition, an addict. Even if he or she is still an apprentice addict. Impaling yourself defies nature.

■ Long ago we gave up the notion that addictions were all about chemicals. Compulsive gamblers showed us that. Since then the concept of addiction has broadened considerably. There are notions of sex addiction. Sometimes men who are habitually unfaithful use that as their defence when they're found out. But I've also seen some men 'addicted' to brothels and some bisexual men 'addicted' to fast, anonymous gay sex before they go back to their unsuspecting wives and kids. Are bulimics 'addicted' to the cream buns on which they binge and gym-junkies 'addicted' to exercise?

■ Finally, the message is getting through to us that the most common addictions have nothing to do with anything smuggled into the country in someone's rectum. The worst drugs are available over the counter of the tobacconist or the bar of your local pub.

So what do you do, as a midlifer, when your kids come home all giggly and raid the fridge? You're just going to have to start talking to them. In benign, non-judgmental, non-freak-out tones. Let them know that this is about your concern for them rather than your desire to control them. If they snigger at that claim you'd better start doing some honest introspection about whether you're too controlling anyway.

Most of the time they've just been smoking marijuana. Yes, they inhale just like you did. While we've gone through the phase of 'Reefer Madness' we've also gone through the phase of considering marijuana harmless. But keep a perspective on things. In terms of havoc wreaked on society and families, marijuana is less harmful than the gin and tonic you'll consume tonight over the television news.

Keep in mind that, if your kids really are addicted to something, you can't forcibly rehabilitate them. They're going to have to do this mostly by themselves. Addictions, like puppies, are not just for Christmas. You never stop being an addict. But it also means that you can't make it all better by next weekend.

Some other thoughts on kids

Favouritism
Consider this
You've got two kids. One is attractive, charming, vivacious, intelligent and loving. The other's not so gifted. In fact he/she is plain, plump and bad-tempered. The swan and the stork. The antelope and the warthog. How could genes mix to create such different results? More importantly, how do you try to love them equally? Because that's what parents instinctively try to do: love them all and avoid favourites.

Now here's a little secret that we midlifers (in fact all parents over all eternity) have tried to hide. Of course all parents will love each of their children in a different way. All parents have their favourites but we try not to show it. Otherwise we end up with situations like Cinderella or King Lear.

In my work I see the tragic results. Children whose parents either clumsily or cruelly displayed their favouritism. The favoured kids grow up intolerable because they become accustomed to being treated as 'special'. At worst they impress as being truly arrogant. The unfavoured kids spend their lives trying to feel 'special'. It's an adjective that frequently echoes around the walls of my consulting room. But in their hearts they feel unloved and unlovable. They try to find an antidote to the poison that runs through their veins: envy. More specifically, *sibling rivalry*. It doesn't stop when they become adults. In fact, they take it to their graves.

Beware the gender divisions. Conventional wisdom is that fathers are closer to daughters and mothers closer to sons. It sounds twee, but there's obviously some truth in it. So how do sons feel loved by their fathers and daughters by the mothers? I've seen families in which there is a clear schism based on the gender of the kids.

Also, spare a thought for the parents of autistic children. What if you try desperately to love your child but get nothing back? After all, loving kids is easy when they hug you in return.

Enjoying kids

Mention of autistic kids brings me to the next simple observation: we parents have kids for rather selfish reasons: we enjoy them. They give us a deep sense of fulfilment and satisfaction, especially if they can stay off the heroin and out of prison.

Our kids pick it up too. They see it in our faces when we talk to them. They hear the pride in our voices when we speak about them to others. They like to have fun with us and we with them. But this doesn't apply to all families ...

■ It's awfully destructive to children's self-esteem to feel that their parents don't like or love them. Children think in a destructively egocentric way. If they feel unloved they automatically presume there's something wrong with them, rather than their parents. They come to the conclusion, consciously or unconsciously, that they must be unlovable, and sometimes even years of psychotherapy doesn't root out this evil conclusion.

- Plenty of my patients have come to a common and tragic realisation: that their parents never praised them, but boasted about them to others. How sad is that?

- The invasion of television into our lives and living rooms has resulted in the lost art of conversation. That's a problem because kids need to be talked and listened to. Even when we parents converse with our kids we tend to be better at talking than at listening. And when it comes to conversing, women seem to be so much better at it than men. We males have to make a special effort to stretch the vocal cords. If we don't make that effort bad things can happen. I've lost count of the number of patients I've encountered who've emphasised within psychotherapy how they grew up feeling unheard. That's another echoing adjective. They're the sort of patients who, once they're into the swing of therapy, are like pigs in mud: for the first time they truly feel listened to.

  In fact kids who feel unheard can feel alone, unloved, unimportant and even invisible. Yes, invisible. Odd but true. If you don't interact with your parents – bounce off them so to speak – you can grow up feeling not only that you're unimportant but that you're nothing. Immaterial. Invisible. Such are the machinations of the juvenile mind.

- Another interesting observation: the parentified child. This usually happens to the oldest child of a larger family. Sometimes the second-oldest kid cops it. The process is that too much responsibility is put onto the oldest kid from too young an age. This can be a seductive role (the 'little mother' or 'little father') but destructive. Kids in this predicament grow up sandwiched between the generations. They're like middle management in a company: they have lots of responsibility but no true authority. The worst consequence is that somewhere in their adulthood they wonder whatever happened to the frivolity and innocence that was supposed to be their childhood. They then tend to fall into the trap of recreating their past by promptly having more kids to look after (so familiar!) or turning their young adulthood into an orgy of the sort of self-indulgence they've missed out on.

Teenagers

'When I was sixteen I thought my father knew nothing. Now that I'm twenty-one I'm surprised how much he's learned in the past five years.'

These words are attributed to Mark Twain. Pity his poor father. But then most teenagers feel this way. We did when we were that age. We knew it all. Midlife gives us the humility to acknowledge that we'll never know it all before the Alzheimer's gets us and then we'll know even less ...

So here are some thoughts about teenagers. First, let me declare that having teenage kids is the most enjoyable phase of bringing up your own brood. Yes, they're utterly selfish, foul-smelling, hormonal, shouting, shrieking, money-grabbing, arrogant creatures who live in bomb-sites they call bedrooms. But on the other hand you can have a semi-reasonable conversation with them. You can have fun with them. They're entertaining. If nothing else, they're never boring. And their saving grace is that they eventually grow up and leave home. Eventually. Then you can truly relate to them as adult-to-adult, even if you never ever stop being their parents.

Fathers, take an extra note of this: you have two special challenges with your teenage sons:

1. You have to show them how to treat a woman. Respect, intimacy and sharing. Too often have I seen the situation in which the battered wife finally throws out the violent husband, only to be beaten up by the adolescent son.

2. You have to do battle with them. They'll get stroppy and you have to retaliate. You both have to shout at each other but keep fists out of the equation even if you'd love to throttle them. One day soon, you see, they'll be big enough to punch you to the ground and there's no faster way to ensure you'll never get on when they're adults. Part of the battle is that you have to lose. Slowly and graciously, but the object of the exercise is not to crush their burgeoning sense of manhood. When they're thirteen or fourteen you have to remind them you're their father and you'll set the rules. When they're fifteen and sixteen you have to try the same approach, but let them win sometimes. By the time they're seventeen or eighteen you no longer have any true control over them, even if you both play a polite game of pretending this to be the case. Until they want to tell you where to go, that is. But take heart, because what you're doing is letting this son of yours be manly.

The 'empty nest'

Right now, in midlife and with a houseful of adolescents, *I can't wait* until they all leave home and strike out on their own journeys through life! I vividly recall the day we brought our first baby home from the maternity hospital. But I wonder how I'll feel on the day our last child packs her bags and waves us goodbye ...

To be honest, I might feel deeply sad, as if another chapter of my life book is closing. It'll confront me with the reality that I don't have that many chapters left. Also, every parent knows that sensation when even one of your children is away and how big, empty and silent the house suddenly seems.

And for couples? The empty nest can put an inordinate strain on marriages, just as any phase of transition can. We human beings like constancy. Logic says that changes for the good should be greeted with relief and celebration and watching your children grow up and individuate must be a change for the good, mustn't it? All that responsibility, all that financial and emotional responsibility just walking out the door. That should be an occasion for red carpets and brass bands, shouldn't it? Maybe not.

Consider this

You're a parent. You're also a hopeless alcoholic. One day, after waking in the police cells once again, you decide to give up the grog. You go to Alcoholics Anonymous and get yourself a whole new group of friends, not just drinking buddies. Your family should be tickled pink by this change in you. Or so you'd think. But sometimes a good change like this can destabilise a family. All of a sudden the new, sober you becomes an identity in the family again, not just someone who snores loudly in the corner of the living room. The family dynamics, the power balance, the chores, the ways of relating are all put into a state of flux. At times your family wishes quietly that you'd just go and 'bust' again with a bottle of vodka so that they could all get back to the *status quo*. To the way it worked, or sort of worked, for all those years before A.A. got to you.

So it is with the 'empty nest'. Just another time of difficult re-adjustment.

I expect that this transition in our lives might be like a grief. On the one hand is the loss of one role and identity which might take some 'working through' as the psycho-jargon goes. On the other hand we'll be able to exult in the removal of all that responsibility. We'll be able to be self-indulgent and irresponsible. Just like teenagers ...

Finally, for the childless (or *child-free*, depending upon your perspective), understand that the moment you or your partner conceive, your life is changed forever in ways that you can't even begin to comprehend right now. So is it worth it? Of course. That's why people keep doing it again and again and again.

CHAPTER 9

IDENTITY

Good work. Congratulations. You've struggled through the chapters about the bio-psycho-social challenges of midlife, from gout to gloom to grotty teenage kids. Now let's get back to the question I skirted around in Chapter 2. In early adulthood you ask yourself the question 'Who will I be?' On your deathbed you ask yourself the question 'Who was I?' Now you're in midlife, *who are you?* What is your *identity*, your *sense of self*? Once you've got this issue beaten, you're on the home run of your midlife turmoil.

This may seem like a lot of airy-fairy navel-gazing, but the issue of identity is probably at the heart of much midlife angst. That's because, in midlife, the sense of self that you've been quite comfortable with for the last few decades suddenly begins to change. There emerges *a jarring incongruity between how you see yourself and how others see you.* They want you to be the old predictable you they've known and loved (or hated) for all these years. You want to reinvent yourself.

Confused? Good. Read on and all will be revealed.

In order to have a sense of self you need four things:

1. a 'census data' identity

2. boundaries

3. memories of where you've come from and who you've been

4. the appropriate use of 'masks'.

A 'CENSUS DATA' IDENTITY

If you ever fill out a form, such as a census form, the first thing you record is your identifying information. Name, rank, serial number, etc. Probing forms may also classify your age group, socio-economic status, religious affiliation, etc. This is the sort of identity that clumps you with so many other people who are similar to you. Not such a big midlife challenge, because these data aren't that contentious. But here's an interesting exercise:

Consider this

You're part of a witness protection program. You've got some criminal jailed for the next twenty years. What a pity he's got a lot of 'extramural' friends who are in a mood to make you pay for what you've done. Baddies don't like squealers and they're already sizing you up for a pair of concrete socks before taking you for a swim in the harbour.

That's when the constabulary step in. You have to take your family and go to a distant city. You have to assume a new name, appearance and career. All those things that previously identified you, even your signature, are now part of the past. Filling out a census form will no longer be something you do without even thinking. You don't like it but you also know that you can't swim and wear concrete at the same time.

So who will you be? What will you call yourself? How will you change your appearance, your style, your work identity?

Sure, midlife is a time for re-inventing yourself, but this is taking it to the extreme.

BOUNDARIES

I touched on this issue in the last chapter. There are all sorts of boundaries:

- Boundaries of your power and authority. Grandiose, arrogant or controlling individuals have problems with these.

- Boundaries of your responsibility, duty, loyalty. Dependent or overly conscientious people have problems with these, as do 'compulsive rescuers'.

- Boundaries of confidentiality, privacy, secrecy or modesty. Know-alls, exhibitionists and gossips have problems with these.

All very well. Now look at these boundaries more closely. They all have an element of narcissism in them, of fantasies of power, of superior knowledge, etc. There's even something narcissistic in people who run around rescuing others. Psychoanalysts view all of these boundaries as relating back to our infancy, when all we had to do was squawk and a large female with a kindly face (our mother) would bring a couple of milk jugs to fill our stomachs and warm, dry diapers to soothe the other end. We came to realise how important and powerful we were. We didn't even have to cook, clean or take ourselves to the bathroom. It was all done for us, for the measly price of a squawk. This was our phase of 'primary narcissism'. Most of us subsequently found out that we weren't really that special. We had to delay gratification, wait our turn and look out for the needs of others. Some of us were spoilt kids and might never have grown out of this phase of self-importance and entitlement. All of us have within us some residue of it.

Midlife is a phase or revision of our boundaries because it's such a humbling experience. As elaborated in Chapter 3, midlife is a phase of meekness and disillusionment. In midlife we can no longer be the Siren or the Adonis. Our fantasies of being the managing director are diluted to hanging onto our job in middle management. When we enlisted we wanted to be the general. Now we'll have to settle for sergeant.

MEMORIES OF WHO YOU'VE BEEN

If you'd opened this book at this chapter you might wonder what the hell I'm going on about. In order to grasp the current ramblings it's handy to have read all the previous ramblings. So it is with our sense of self: it relies on a continuous set of memories. Our history and tradition. That's why we hang onto our wedding photos and embarrass our kids by producing a camera at their birthday parties.

Imagine this

You wake up in a bed in a room. You have no idea how you got here or, for that matter, where you are. That's not as horrifying as the next realisation: you have no memory at all up until the present moment. To be precise, you have no idea who you are. Or where you've come from. You look down at your hands, your torso, your legs. You've never seen them before. You might as well be looking over the shoulder of a stranger. There's a mirror in the room so you rush to it. You gasp as you see this face that looks back at you.

This is the stuff of science fiction movies. Don't fret. As long as you hang onto your gray matter and don't drink it away you'll probably never have to encounter this particular horror. But it does give an interesting insight into just how important our sense of self is. Most of us, if we had to endure this total amnesia, would find the experience devastating. Our identity, like our health, is something we tend to take for granted.

THE APPROPRIATE USE OF 'MASKS'

We all wear them. They're the faces and graces we put on when we're playing a role, which we're doing most of our waking hours. We relate to a shop assistant with one mask, our accountant with another, unruly kids with a parental mask, flirtatious people with a seductive mask and traffic police with a mask that broadcasts innocence and regret. Our neighbours think they know us but they only know our neighbourly mask. When we play with our kids we give them a glimpse behind our adult mask at the eternal child within.

My own role as a psychiatrist is to try to see beyond the masks that are presented to me, or to create such an air of mutual trust that people don't mind leaving their masks in the waiting room.

Usually we really only remove our masks with those we know and love. Our spouses know us mask-free and somehow manage to put up with us. When we take our clothes off in front of someone we generally take our masks off at the same time.

Now there are a number of problems with masks. What if you remove your masks and there's nothing left? What if you find that, if you're not playing some sort of role, you have no sense of who you are? Some people endure this awful experience daily.

In midlife there's often a real internal struggle when we come to appreciate that there's an incongruity between how we see ourselves and how others see us. Nothing is more disquieting than having to create a False Self.

Consider this

You're a man but you don't feel that way. You were brought up as a little boy. The problem is that you've always known you were a little girl trapped in a male body. Now you're an adult you go through the motions of being a bloke. You drink beer and belong to a pistol club. You dress in dowdy fashions. You learn how to spit and swear. You even learn how to have sex with women even if this feels, well, odd.

Inside you know you're a woman. The Jarring Incongruity. The disquiet of the False Self.

Later in life you institute your own witness protection program by moving to a distant city. You dress as a woman and change your name from Ron to something more ladylike. The jarring and disquiet start to ease. But they're really put to rest by the surgery that removes the discrepant organ. If thy penis offends thee, cut it off ...

This is an extreme example to illustrate a point. Another example might be the so-called Banana Syndrome. You're Asian but brought up in a Western culture. You feel yellow on the outside but white on the inside. A further example may be if you're gay and must go through the motions of acting like a 'breeder' in order to avoid mockery or rejection.

In midlife our sense of self changes so rapidly and so profoundly it can be jarring. Midlife is a time of truth and abandonment of self-deception. We find that our old masks and roles don't suit us anymore. We cast off fantasies of being anyone other than Us. We become more accepting of who we've turned out to be rather than wishing to assume loftier identities. The need to admire role models falls by the wayside. We want to be ourselves and to be accepted as ourselves. To pretend to no one and have no other identities foisted upon us. We get sick of False Selves.

The question keeps coming up again and again. Who am I? When we stop asking the question we've usually settled into a much greater comfort with our own identity. When we stop asking the question we've found our True Self. We're through midlife and onto the next phase.

CHAPTER 10

MORTALITY

Young people often attract another adjective that questions their wisdom: 'young and silly' is the expression. Young people ride motorcycles and go to war. They really have no true concept of their own mortality. It's just an abstract noun that happens to other people, especially baddies in the movies. Or unfortunate masses in the Third World. It's too far away to have any true meaning for them. That's why they're so completely unprepared for war and return jaded, having overdosed on reality. But that's also why they're sent to war. We midlifers know too much. We'd do anything we could to avoid it. As Oscar Wilde once said: 'There's nothing like an execution in the morning to sharpen the wits of the condemned man.'

Midlife is a time of confronting the reality and inevitability of our own deaths. At some stage we midlifers have looked at a frail, gray, doddery old person, so unattractive in our lexicon of studs and supermodels, and truly realised we'll be like that one day soon. We're so busy. Time passes quickly. The next thing we know, we're eligible for the pension.

And in the process of our noses being rubbed in notions of mortality, we also struggle, like never before, to find a meaning for our lives.

QUIZ

After you die, what happens?

1. You go somewhere. It might be heaven or hell or, depending upon which religion got hold of you in your infancy, purgatory. Once in heaven or hell you stay there forever, even if time has no particular meaning in that state.

2. Nothing happens. Death's the end. No more awareness or sense of self. Nowhere to go. You leave behind bones and memories of you in the minds of your loved ones, neither of which survive very long. Even your gravestone will eventually erode and crumble. If you're particularly lucky (or unlucky perhaps) some archaeologist will disturb your grave in several aeons' time and wonder who you were. Not a lot of consolation.

3. You're reincarnated. One moment you're in the hospice gasping for breath, the next moment you're a mosquito giving me grief on some dusty road near Marrakesh. To come back as a mosquito you must've been a bit of a ratbag the last time around. After I've slapped the life out of you you're reborn as a lamb on some hillside in Argentina. Good luck on your long road to nirvana and the escape from recurring cycles of suffering.

4. You're as honest with yourself as you could possibly be. You have to admit you have no idea what happens after death. You wish someone could 'come back', like Marco Polo, and regale you with stories of the adventure. In the meantime you'll settle for what you have to do rather than what you'd like to do. You'd like to live forever but you know you have to face death one day. Then you'll know.

5. You feel you go somewhere but the notions of heaven and hell seem a little too contrived. You don't really think you'll be reunited with your old earthly body on the Last Day (you never really did like that body anyway) and you can't bend your head around places that have either streets of gold (a great way to devalue bullion) or eternal flames (just think of the gas bill!). You have a sense of the Divine in your life so you'll trust in Him or It. You're quite sure there's an afterlife but in some form that's incomprehensible. Even if an adventurer made it back he'd be unable to describe it to you .

Now here's another scary question: what does it feel like to die? Our greatest fantasy is to die in our sleep. To nod off one night and wake up to ... well, whatever it is that happens next. Perfect. For most people death comes suddenly and seems reasonably gentle. This applies, of course, to heart attacks and strokes that are big enough to finish you off. Little, disabling strokes and heart attacks are a complete nuisance unless you make a startling recovery from them.

Cancer is our big fear, for obvious reasons. If it has any advantage at all it's that you have time to say goodbye to people. That presumes that you're not so scared you have to go into denial. Also, keep in mind that you'd better say your farewells and 'settle your affairs', as they say, before the morphine makes you unable to do so.

In medical practice I've encountered death often. I've had the humbling experience and the honour of watching people die as I've held their pale hands. I've handed swathed dead babies to their grieving mothers. Medical school innoculates students to death. It's a time-honoured tradition called the Anatomy Laboratory. As a teenager you're introduced to a cadaver (a corpse), which you then slowly dismantle over the next year or two. System by system, organ by organ. It sounds a little grotesque, but it certainly familiarises you with death.

If I can give you any advice about how to have a nice death (if such a thing exists), think about these:

■ Get the best medical care for your death. You tend to think of doctors as being those people who try to save lives. Nothing could be further from the truth. Medicine isn't about saving lives, it's about easing suffering. You also probably think you need a competent medical team to fight the illnesses from which you're going to recover. But I've seen people die in pain because the medical or nursing staff have been too mean with the morphine or too busy or too unfeeling. Before Thomas More was beheaded he paid the executioner to do a good job. When the time comes for your own exit from the mortal coil make sure you've got a caring team who don't try to economise on the painkillers.

■ Make a Living Will. I'm not talking about how you want your assets divided up after you curl up your toes. A Living Will is an agreement you come to with your doctors about how much medical intervention you want when you're terminally ill. Nothing's worse than having a perfectly good death when some young doctor on a power trip comes along to resuscitate you. I've seen it done. Ask your general practitioner about a Living Will. Search the Internet for more information. There are organisations around that espouse this idea and you need to have a chat with them.

There, now that you're more comfortable with your own mortality, you're well and truly beginning to wrap up your midlife.

CHAPTER 11

WHAT NOW?

Now that you know what midlife is, and what havoc it wreaks on your life, you need to follow some steps to get through it. These are:

1. Hang on. Midlife is a bucking bronco but when the ride is finished you and your backside will be relieved and thankful.

2. Be patient. Midlife is one of Nature's cruel jokes, like the observation that you get your libido about five years before you can handle it. And you get your wealth and wisdom at the end of your adult life but you really could have used it at the beginning. So it is with midlife. Don't try to understand it. Just live it.

3. If you're pre-midlife or in early midlife, start planning now. Your sabbatical, how you'll handle those seven midlife fantasies, how to control those uncontrollable adolescent kids, how you're going to escape this stultifying job, how you're going to do more exercise, what you're going to do when you hit the 'empty nest' phase, where you're going to keep your Living Will and who the good geriatricians and psychiatrists are in your town.

4. Grow old disgracefully. You're going to be dead for a long time and no one will remember those scandalous things you got away with in your forties.

5. Make fun, play and humour an everyday experience.

And how will you know when you're over midlife? When does it stop? When your value system has changed to something that's more real and easy. When you use things and love people, not the other way around. When you can go to the beach and enjoy the sun on your skin without caring what anyone else thinks of your bulges. When life has less worry and more self-indulgent enjoyment. When you can look back on your life with less self-criticism and more smug self-satisfaction. When the notion of dying still sits uneasily with you but you know you'll handle it when the time comes. When the notion of ageing doesn't frighten you any more.

∞ ∞ ∞ ∞ ∞ ∞ ∞ ∞ ∞ ∞

That's when you know you're through midlife.